BRAIN TRAINING PUZZLES

BRAIN TRAINING PUZZLES

Over 150 stimulating puzzles

This edition published in 2022 by Arcturus Publishing Limited
26/27 Bickels Yard, 151–153 Bermondsey Street,
London SE1 3HA

AD010221NT

Printed in the UK

Contents

Puzzles:

1 

Domino Placement

A standard set of 28 dominoes has been laid out as shown. Can you draw in the edges of them all?

The check-box is provided as an aid, so that you can see which dominoes have been located.

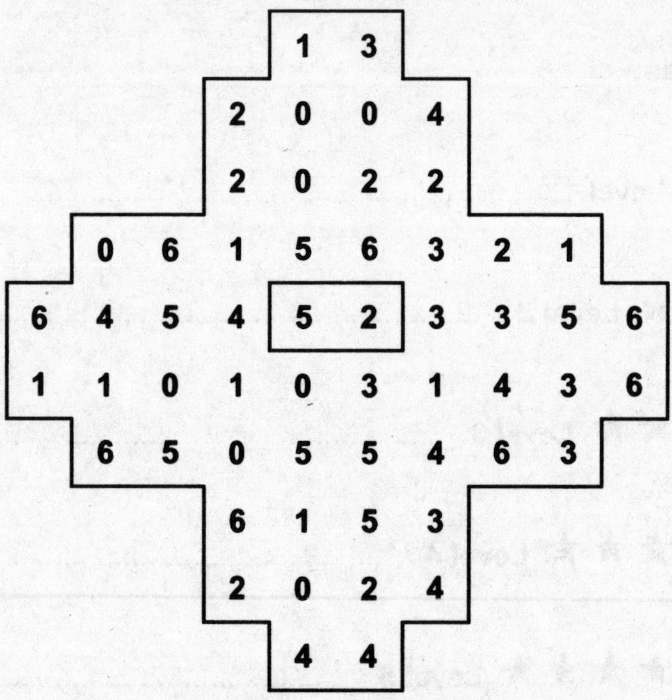

0-0	0-1	0-2	0-3	0-4	0-5	0-6	1-1	1-2	1-3	1-4	1-5	1-6	2-2

2-3	2-4	2-5	2-6	3-3	3-4	3-5	3-6	4-4	4-5	4-6	5-5	5-6	6-6
		✓											

2

Hidato

Starting at 1 and finishing at 36, track your way from one square to another, either horizontally, vertically, or diagonally, placing consecutive numbers into the empty squares as you go.

33			8		12
	36	7		10	
31	5		2	15	14
	29			1	
		23			
26	27	24	22	18	19

3

Sum Total

Fill each empty square so that every row contains ten different numbers from 0 to 9. In columns the numbers may be repeated, but wherever one square touches another, whether horizontally, vertically, or diagonally, the numbers must be different. Some are already in place.

The black squares show the sum total of the numbers in each column.

	8		4		9		1		
2		7		5		3		4	1
		3	0		9		6		
7		2			3	4		1	0
2		3	1	0		7	8	9	4
24	33	15	22	15	26	23	28	27	12

Number Link

Working from one square to another, horizontally or vertically (never diagonally), draw single continuous paths to pair up each set of two matching numbers.

No line may cross another, none may travel through any square containing a number, and every square must be visited just once.

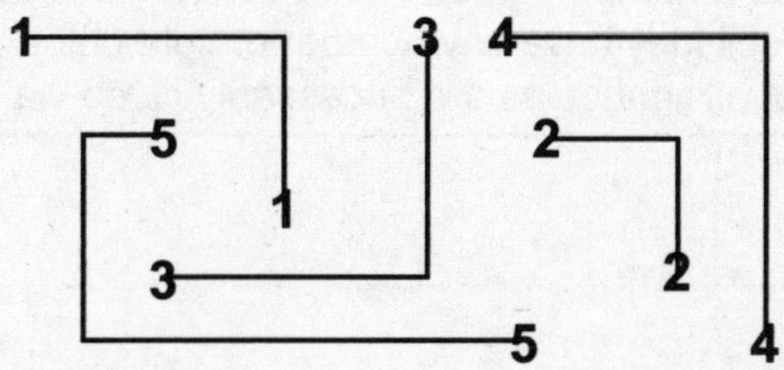

1					2	4	9
7		5				4	9
		7		1			
	3		3				
			5		8		
			6			10	
6	10					8	2

5

Light Up

Place circles (representing light bulbs) in some of the empty squares, in such a way that no two bulbs shine on each other, until every square of the grid is lit up. A bulb sends rays of light horizontally and vertically, illuminating its entire row and column unless its light is blocked by a black cell.

Some black cells contain numbers, indicating how many light bulbs are in adjacent squares either immediately above, below, to the right, or to the left. Bulbs placed diagonally adjacent to a numbered cell do not contribute to the bulb count. An unnumbered black cell may have any number of light bulbs adjacent to it, or none at all, and not all light bulbs are necessarily clued via black squares.

1	1				
	2			0	
		2			
				0	
				0	
	1		1		

Skyscrapers

Place the numbers 1 to 5 into each row and column, one number per square. Each number represents a skyscraper of that many floors.

Arrange the skyscrapers in such a way that the given number outside the grid represents the number of buildings which can be seen from that point, looking only at that number's row or column.

A skyscraper with a lower number of floors cannot hide a higher building, but a one with a higher number of floors always hides any building behind it.

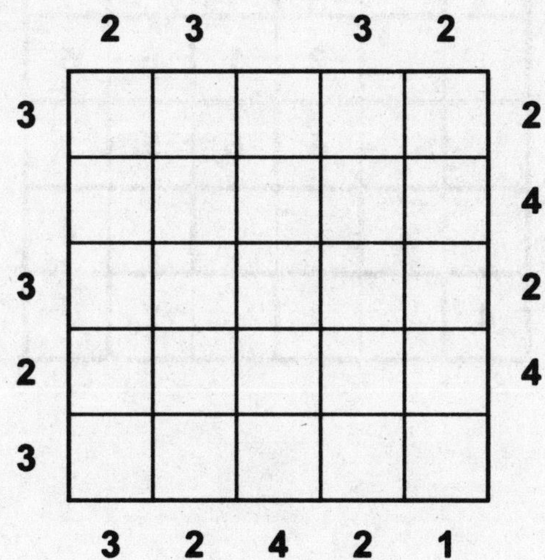

7

Brickwork

Every square should be filled with a number from 1 to 6.
No number may appear twice in any row or column.

Every brick that consists of two squares contains
both an odd number and an even number.

2	5	3		1	
			3		
		2	1	6	5
		4	6	5	
					4
4				2	

8

No Three in Line

Place either O or X into each empty square, so that no three consecutive squares in either a horizontal row or vertical column contain more than two of the same symbol.
There needs to be as many Os as Xs in every row and column.

		O	X				
O			O			X	X
	X					X	
	O				O		X
O				O	X	X	O
	O	X		X			
X						X	O
X	X		X	O		O	O

9

Combiku

Each horizontal row and vertical column should contain four different shapes, and four different numbers.

Every square will contain one number and one shape, and no combination may be repeated anywhere else in the puzzle; so, for instance, if a square contains a 3 and a star, then no other square containing a 3 will also contain a star, and no other square with a star will also contain a 3.

1 **2** **3** **4**

	4		
2	3		
3			

10

Logi-5

Every row and column of this grid should contain one each of the letters A, B, C, D, and E.

In addition, each of the five shapes (marked by thicker lines) should also contain one each of the letters A, B, C, D, and E.

Can you complete the grid?

			C	A
	E	A		C
C		D		
				B
A	C			

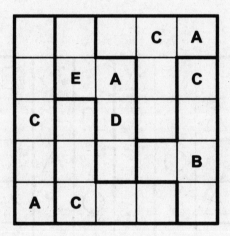

Shape Sorter

The grid below is divided into regions of three squares. Some need to contain three different shapes: a circle, a square, and a triangle; others need to contain three identical shapes.

When two squares share a side across a region boundary, the shapes must be different.

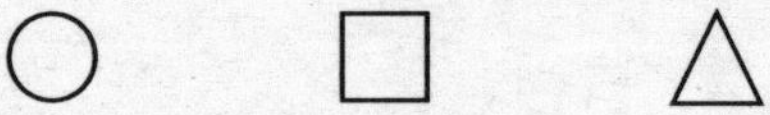

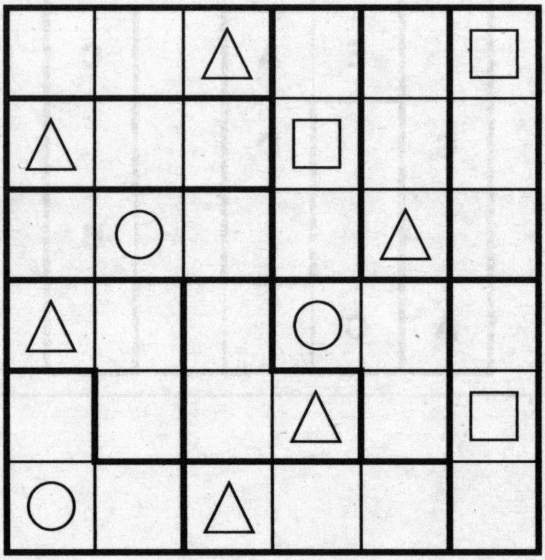

Chains

Fill each empty circle with one of the numbers 1-6.

Every horizontal row, vertical column, set of six linked circles, and diagonal line of six circles should contain six different numbers.

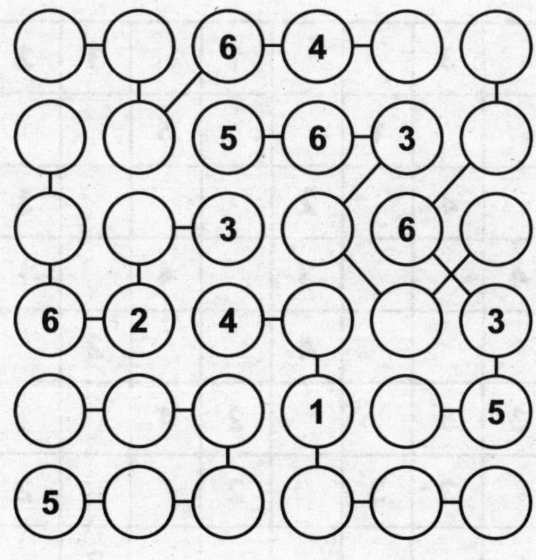

Coin Collecting

In this puzzle, an amateur coin collector has been out with his metal detector, searching for booty. He didn't have time to dig up all the coins he found, so has made a grid map, showing their locations, in the hope that if he loses the map, at least no-one else will understand it... However, he didn't count on YOU coming across the strange grid (as seen here). Will you be able to discover the correct number of coins and their precise locations?

Those squares containing numbers are empty, but where a number appears in a square, it indicates how many coins are located in the squares (up to a maximum of eight) surrounding the numbered one, touching it at any corner or side. There is only one coin in any individual square.

Place a circle into every square containing a coin.

	3			1		3	2
		1			5		
	4		2				3
4			3		4		1
			4			2	
3	5			2	1		
	3	3		2			2
1						2	

14

Patchwork

Every square should be filled with a letter from A to D, and each heavily outlined set of four squares should contain four different letters. Every row and column must contain two of each letter.

Squares that share a common border may not contain the same letter.

C							
			C			D	
B	C	D				B	
C						C	
B			A			A	B
				A	C		
	C			D	B		
A			D	B	A		C

15

Slitherlink

Draw a single continuous loop, by connecting the dots.
No line may cross the path of another.

The figure inside each set of any four surrounding dots indicates the total number of surrounding lines.

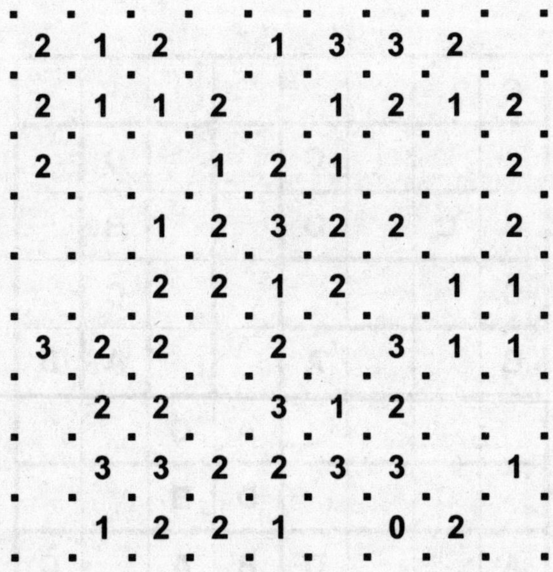

16

Calcudoku

Each row and column should contain six different numbers from 1 to 6.

The numbers placed in a heavily outlined set of squares may be repeated, but must produce the calculation in the top left corner, using the mathematical symbol provided: multiply (x), divide (/), add (+), and subtract (–).

For example, when multiplied, the numbers 4 and 3 total 12:

12x **4**	**3**

12+	15x			14+	10x
	1–	6/			
			7+	96x	
3+	2/			15x	
	2/		7+		
30x				4+	

Bridges

Join the circular islands by drawing horizontal or vertical lines to represent bridges, in such a way that the number of bridges connected to each island must match the number on that island. No bridge may cross another, and no more than two bridges can join any pair of islands.

The finished design will allow you to travel from one island to any other island on the map.

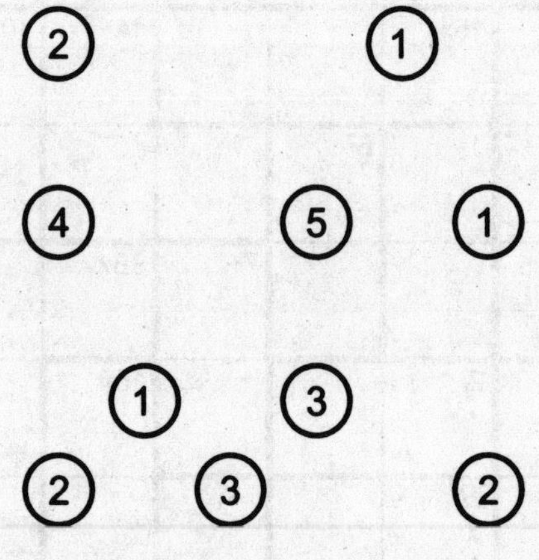

18

No Four in Line

Place either O or X into each empty square, so that no four consecutive squares in a straight line in any direction (horizontally, vertically, or diagonally) contain more than three of the same symbol.

X	X	X		X		O	O	
	X	X		O		O	O	X
			X					O
X	O					X		O
O		O		X			X	
		O	O				O	
	O		O			X	O	
X					O	X	X	O
	O	O	O				X	O

Battleships

Can you place the vessels into the diagram? A number to the right or below a row or column refers to the number of occupied squares in that row or column.

Any vessel may be positioned horizontally or vertically, but no part of a vessel touches part of any other vessel, either horizontally, vertically, or diagonally.

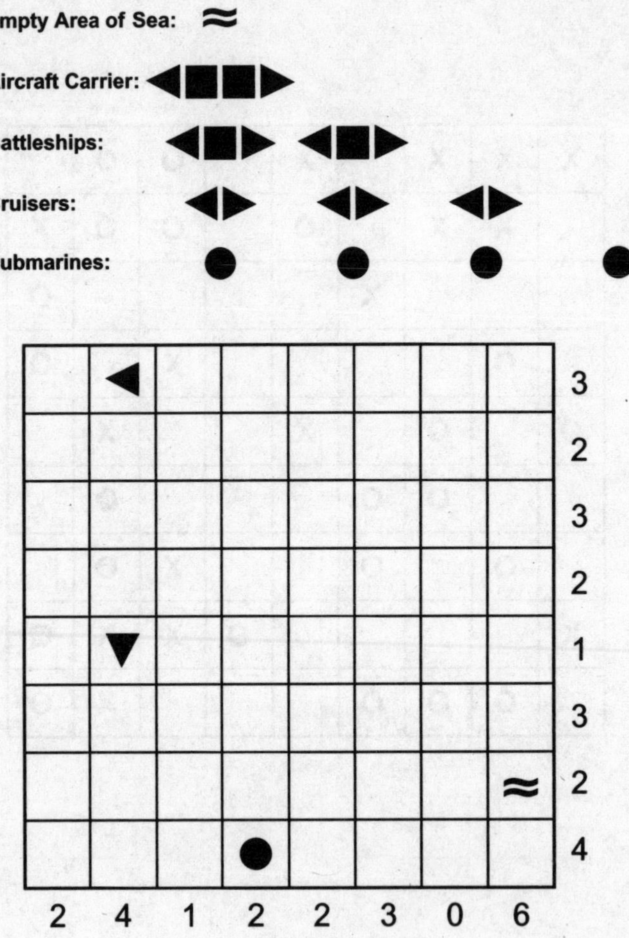

Futoshiki

Fill the grid so that every horizontal row and vertical column contains all the numbers 1 to 6.

Any arrows in the grid always point toward a square that contains a lower number.

^ v > <

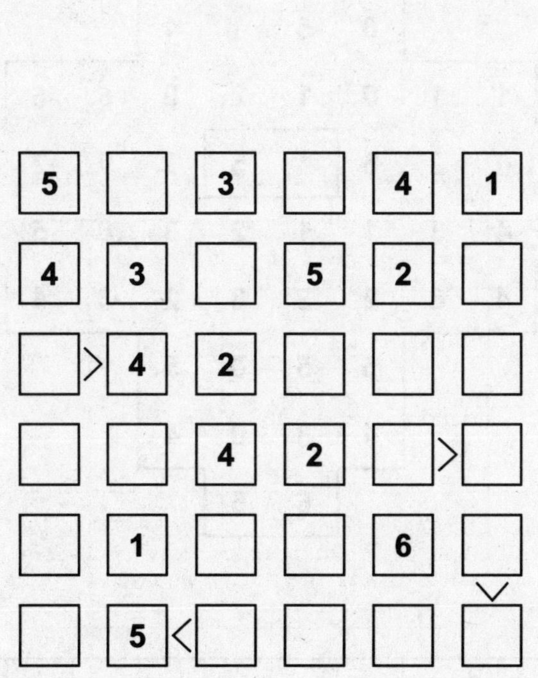

21

Domino Placement

A standard set of 28 dominoes has been laid out as shown. Can you draw in the edges of them all?

The check-box is provided as an aid, so that you can see which dominoes have been located.

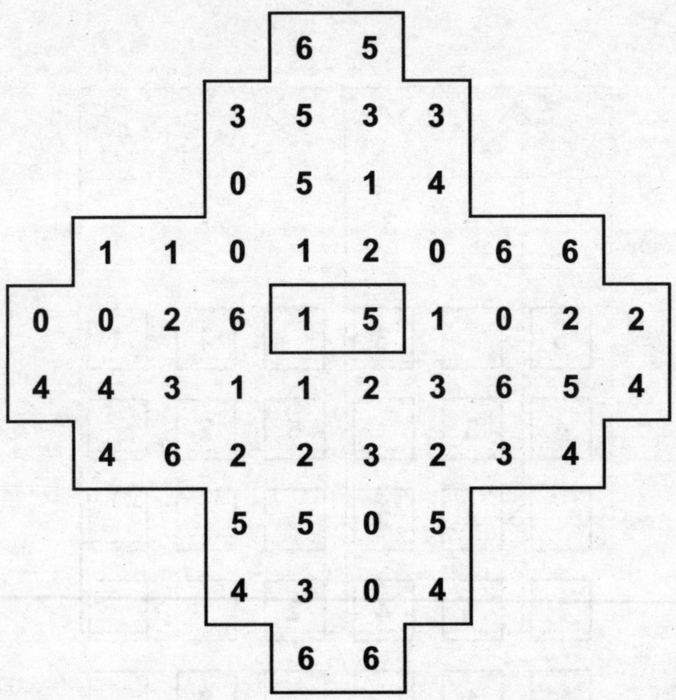

0-0	0-1	0-2	0-3	0-4	0-5	0-6	1-1	1-2	1-3	1-4	1-5	1-6	2-2
											✓		

2-3	2-4	2-5	2-6	3-3	3-4	3-5	3-6	4-4	4-5	4-6	5-5	5-6	6-6

22

Hidato

Starting at 1 and finishing at 36, track your way from one square to another, either horizontally, vertically, or diagonally, placing consecutive numbers into the empty squares as you go.

1	31		29		6
		3		28	
35		11		8	
	36		10		26
15		13		25	21
	17	18	24	23	

23

Sum Total

Fill each empty square so that every row contains ten different numbers from 0 to 9. In columns the numbers may be repeated, but wherever one square touches another, whether horizontally, vertically, or diagonally, the numbers must be different. Some are already in place.

The black squares show the sum total of the numbers in each column.

2	9	4	3		1				
8			9	2	7	5			
		8			3			9	5
		3	7	1		5			2
	4			5	2			8	7
18	26	17	28	22	21	17	26	30	20

24

Number Link

Working from one square to another, horizontally or vertically (never diagonally), draw single continuous paths to pair up each set of two matching numbers.

No line may cross another, none may travel through any square containing a number, and every square must be visited just once.

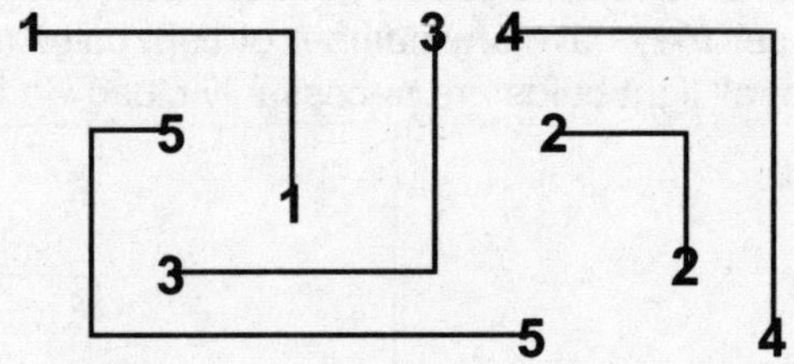

<table>
<tr><td>4</td><td></td><td></td><td></td><td></td><td></td><td></td><td></td></tr>
<tr><td></td><td></td><td></td><td></td><td></td><td></td><td>6</td><td></td></tr>
<tr><td></td><td>1</td><td></td><td></td><td>4</td><td></td><td></td><td></td></tr>
<tr><td></td><td></td><td>5</td><td></td><td></td><td></td><td></td><td></td></tr>
<tr><td>2</td><td></td><td></td><td></td><td></td><td></td><td></td><td></td></tr>
<tr><td></td><td></td><td></td><td></td><td></td><td>3</td><td></td><td></td></tr>
<tr><td>2</td><td></td><td></td><td>5</td><td></td><td></td><td></td><td></td></tr>
<tr><td>6</td><td></td><td>3</td><td>1</td><td></td><td></td><td></td><td></td></tr>
</table>

Light Up

Place circles (representing light bulbs) in some of the empty squares, in such a way that no two bulbs shine on each other, until every square of the grid is lit up. A bulb sends rays of light horizontally and vertically, illuminating its entire row and column unless its light is blocked by a black cell.

Some black cells contain numbers, indicating how many light bulbs are in adjacent squares either immediately above, below, to the right, or to the left. Bulbs placed diagonally adjacent to a numbered cell do not contribute to the bulb count. An unnumbered black cell may have any number of light bulbs adjacent to it, or none at all, and not all light bulbs are necessarily clued via black squares.

26

Skyscrapers

Place the numbers 1 to 5 into each row and column, one number per square. Each number represents a skyscraper of that many floors.

Arrange the skyscrapers in such a way that the given number outside the grid represents the number of buildings which can be seen from that point, looking only at that number's row or column.

A skyscraper with a lower number of floors cannot hide a higher building, but one with a higher number of floors always hides any building behind it.

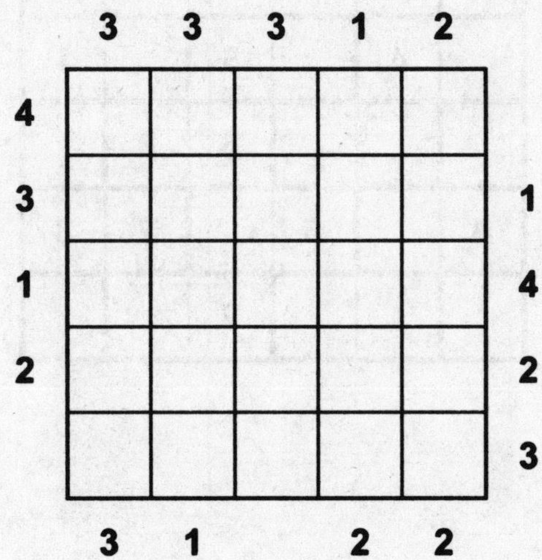

27

Brickwork

Every square should be filled with a number from 1 to 6. No number may appear twice in any row or column.

Every brick that consists of two squares contains both an odd number and an even number.

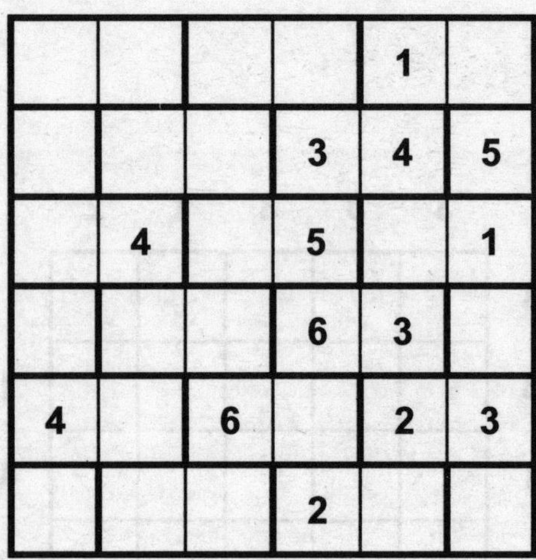

28

No Three in Line

Place either O or X into each empty square, so that no three consecutive squares in either a horizontal row or vertical column contain more than two of the same symbol.

There needs to be as many Os as Xs in every row and column.

	O		O	X		X	
X		O	O			X	O
					X		
		X	X		O	X	
						O	O
			X	O			
X		O		O		O	O
X	X		O			O	

Combiku

Each horizontal row and vertical column should contain four different shapes, and four different numbers.

Every square will contain one number and one shape, and no combination may be repeated anywhere else in the puzzle; so, for instance, if a square contains a 3 and a star, then no other square containing a 3 will also contain a star, and no other square with a star will also contain a 3.

1 2 3 4

4		1	
	1		4
	2		3

Logi-5

Every row and column of this grid should contain one each of the letters A, B, C, D, and E.

In addition, each of the five shapes (marked by thicker lines) should also contain one each of the letters A, B, C, D, and E.

Can you complete the grid?

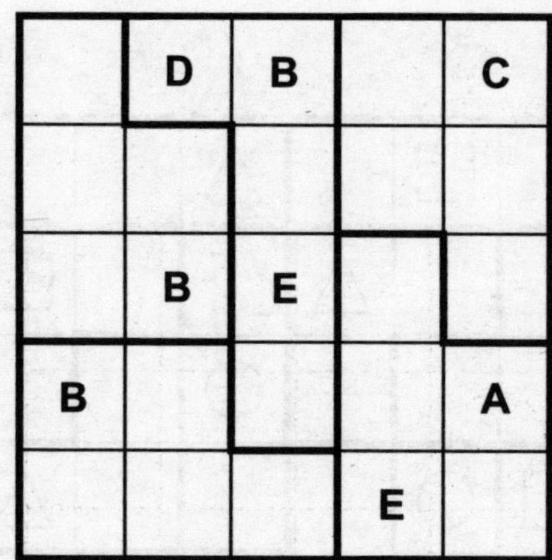

	D	B		C
	B	E		
B				A
			E	

31

Shape Sorter

The grid below is divided into regions of three squares. Some need to contain three different shapes: a circle, a square, and a triangle; others need to contain three identical shapes.

When two squares share a side across a region boundary, the shapes must be different.

○ □ △

	□		△		
△		△			□
			○		
□	○				△
			□		
		△			○

Chains

Fill each empty circle with one of the numbers 1-6.

Every horizontal row, vertical column, set of six linked circles, and diagonal line of six circles should contain six different numbers.

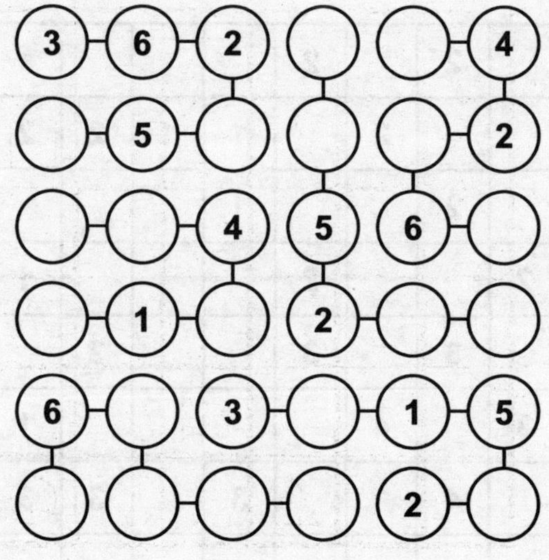

33

Coin Collecting

In this puzzle, an amateur coin collector has been out with his metal detector, searching for booty. He didn't have time to dig up all the coins he found, so has made a grid map, showing their locations, in the hope that if he loses the map, at least no-one else will understand it... However, he didn't count on YOU coming across the strange grid (as seen here). Will you be able to discover the correct number of coins and their precise locations?

Those squares containing numbers are empty, but where a number appears in a square, it indicates how many coins are located in the squares (up to a maximum of eight) surrounding the numbered one, touching it at any corner or side. There is only one coin in any individual square.

Place a circle into every square containing a coin.

	2		2				
		2		1	1	2	2
	2			1			
2			2				1
	3		3			2	
3		4					1
	4			3		3	3
			1				

34

Patchwork

Every square should be filled with a letter from A to E, and each heavily outlined set of five squares should contain five different letters. Every row and column must contain two of each letter.

Squares that share a common border may not contain the same letter.

C		E	D			D		E	
	C		B				A		
		E		D		B			
									D
E					C		D		A
B	C	B			D				
	D	C					C		
	B		C						A
	D		E	B			B		
B				D	B		D		C

35

Slitherlink

Draw a single continuous loop, by connecting the dots. No line may cross the path of another.

The figure inside each set of any four surrounding dots indicates the total number of surrounding lines.

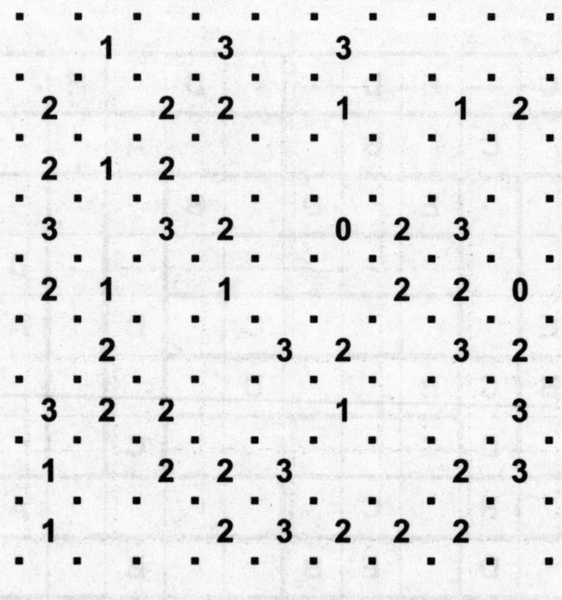

36

Calcudoku

Each row and column should contain six different numbers from 1 to 6.

The numbers placed in a heavily outlined set of squares may be repeated, but must produce the calculation in the top left corner, using the mathematical symbol provided: multiply (x), divide (/), add (+), and subtract (–).

For example, when multiplied, the numbers 4 and 3 total 12:

12x 4	3

8x			7+	15x	
10+		6x		20x	18x
5x	6x		20x		
				12x	
13+		3–			5+
	1–		1–		

37

Bridges

Join the circular islands by drawing horizontal or vertical lines to represent bridges, in such a way that the number of bridges connected to each island must match the number on that island. No bridge may cross another, and no more than two bridges can join any pair of islands.

The finished design will allow you to travel from one island to any other island on the map.

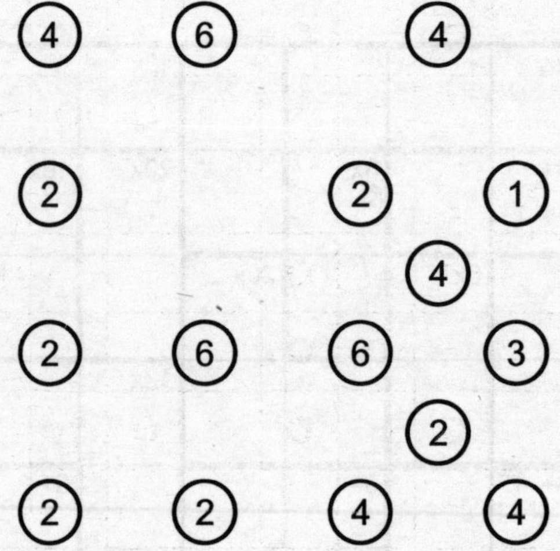

38

No Four in Line

Place either O or X into each empty square, so that no four consecutive squares in a straight line in any direction (horizontally, vertically, or diagonally) contain more than three of the same symbol.

X	O			X				O
		O		O		O		X
X						O	O	O
	X		X					
O				O				O
O			O	O				
O		O		O		O		X
								X
X		X		X			X	X

Battleships

Can you place the vessels into the diagram? A number to the right or below a row or column refers to the number of occupied squares in that row or column.

Any vessel may be positioned horizontally or vertically, but no part of a vessel touches part of any other vessel, either horizontally, vertically, or diagonally.

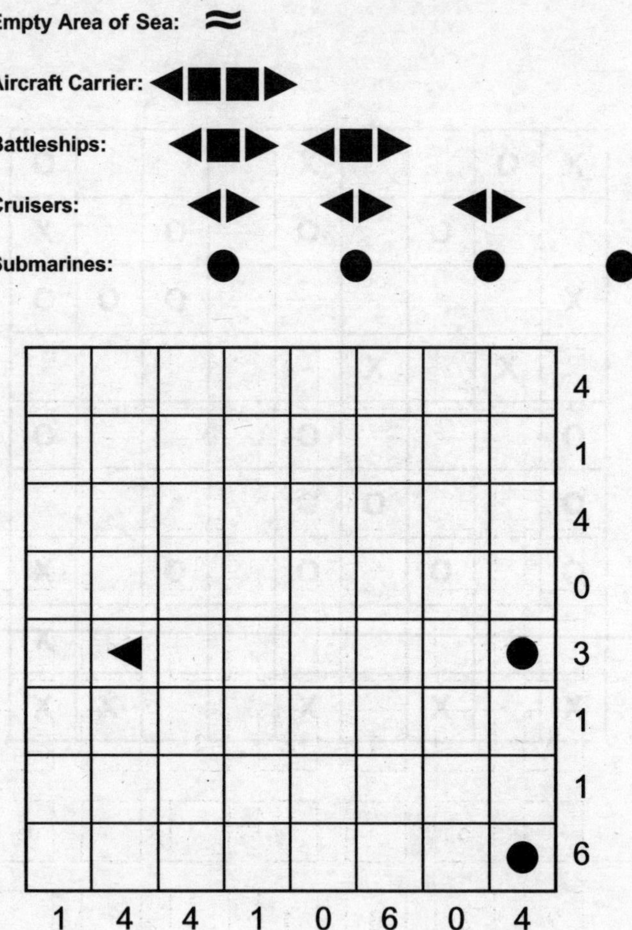

40

Futoshiki

Fill the grid so that every horizontal row and vertical column contains all the numbers 1 to 7.

Any arrows in the grid always point toward a square that contains a lower number.

∧ ∨ > <

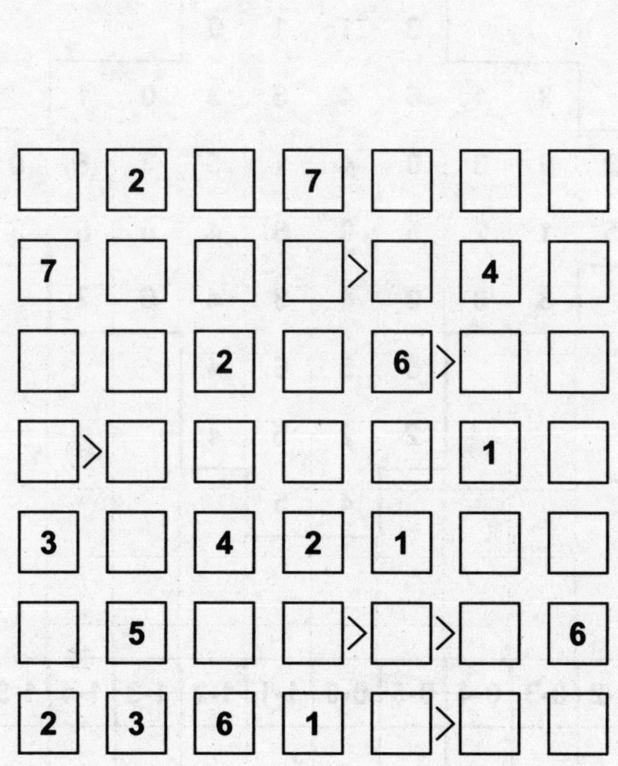

Domino Placement

A standard set of 28 dominoes has been laid out as shown. Can you draw in the edges of them all?

The check-box is provided as an aid, so that you can see which dominoes have been located.

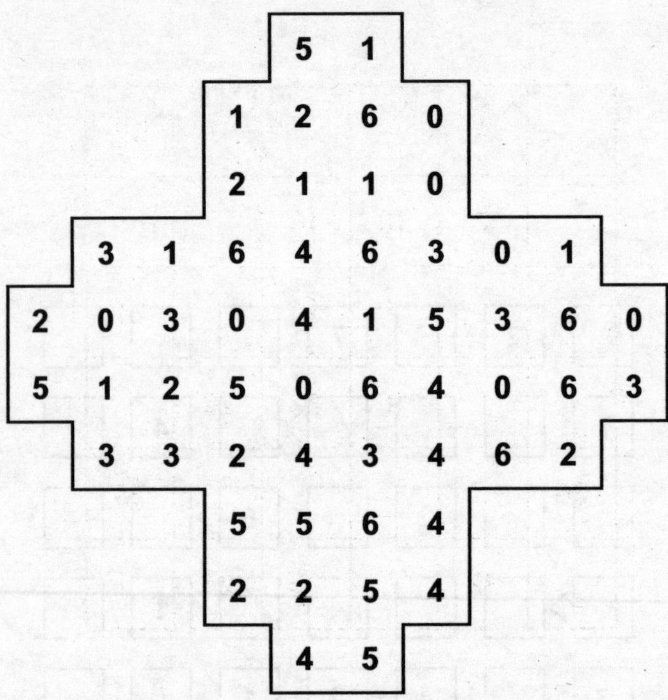

0-0	0-1	0-2	0-3	0-4	0-5	0-6	1-1	1-2	1-3	1-4	1-5	1-6	2-2

2-3	2-4	2-5	2-6	3-3	3-4	3-5	3-6	4-4	4-5	4-6	5-5	5-6	6-6

42

Hidato

Starting at 1 and finishing at 36, track your way from one square to another, either horizontally, vertically, or diagonally, placing consecutive numbers into the empty squares as you go.

	4				12
	2	16	18		
1		7	10		21
		9	23	22	
36					28
	32		25	26	

43

Sum Total

Fill each empty square so that every row contains ten different numbers from 0 to 9. In columns the numbers may be repeated, but wherever one square touches another, whether horizontally, vertically, or diagonally, the numbers must be different. Some are already in place.

The black squares show the sum total of the numbers in each column.

	0	5		4			1	3	
			9		5	2			
0	2	1					8		
5		9		3	1			4	
4				5			9		0
16	19	20	28	27	23	24	26	29	13

Number Link

Working from one square to another, horizontally or vertically (never diagonally), draw single continuous paths to pair up each set of two matching numbers.

No line may cross another, none may travel through any square containing a number, and every square must be visited just once.

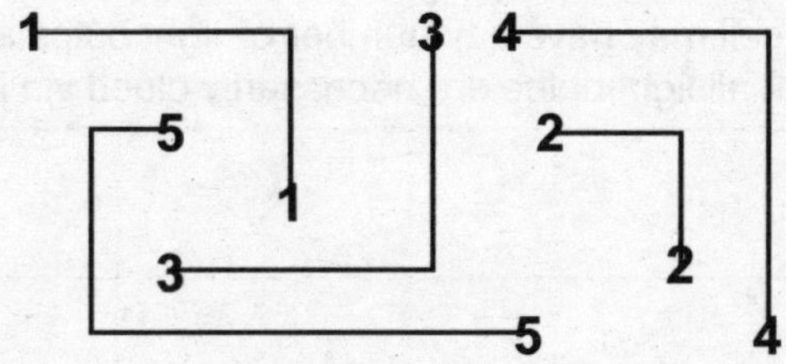

				6			6	1
		5		12	1			
12		2	10					
2				7	11		11	
		5					7	
					8	3		10
					4			
	9		9		13		4	
8	13				3			

Light Up

Place circles (representing light bulbs) in some of the empty squares, in such a way that no two bulbs shine on each other, until every square of the grid is lit up. A bulb sends rays of light horizontally and vertically, illuminating its entire row and column unless its light is blocked by a black cell.

Some black cells contain numbers, indicating how many light bulbs are in adjacent squares either immediately above, below, to the right, or to the left. Bulbs placed diagonally adjacent to a numbered cell do not contribute to the bulb count. An unnumbered black cell may have any number of light bulbs adjacent to it, or none at all, and not all light bulbs are necessarily clued via black squares.

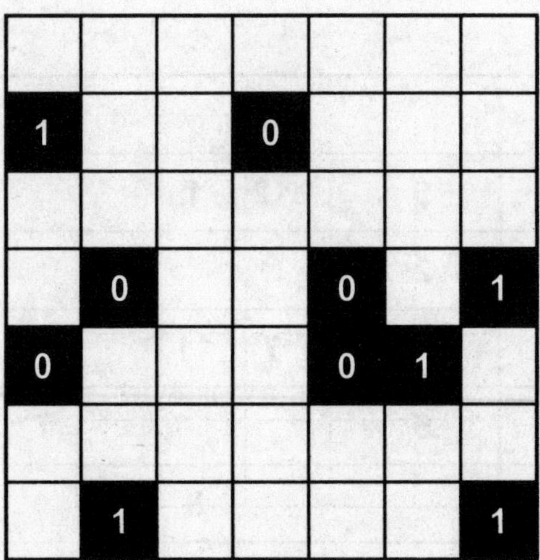

46

Skyscrapers

Place the numbers 1 to 5 into each row and column, one number per square. Each number represents a skyscraper of that many floors.

Arrange the skyscrapers in such a way that the given number outside the grid represents the number of buildings which can be seen from that point, looking only at that number's row or column.

A skyscraper with a lower number of floors cannot hide a higher building, but a one with a higher number of floors always hides any building behind it.

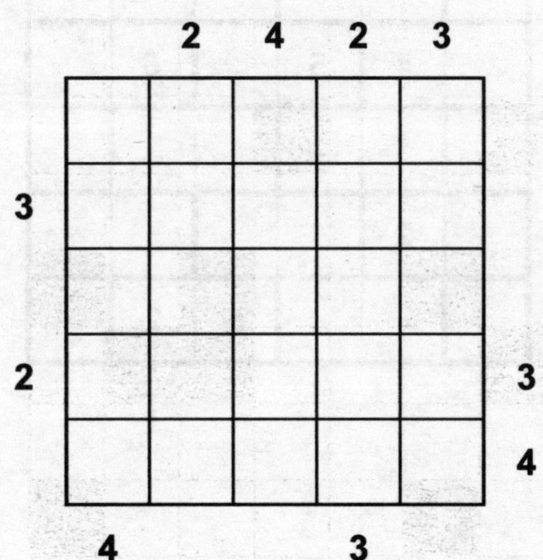

Brickwork

Every square should be filled with a number from 1 to 6.
No number may appear twice in any row or column.

Every brick that consists of two squares contains
both an odd number and an even number.

4					6
			3		
	4	5		6	
	1				
	2				
			5	2	

48

No Three in Line

Place either O or X into each empty square, so that no three consecutive squares in either a horizontal row or vertical column contain more than two of the same symbol. There needs to be as many Os as Xs in every row and column.

X							
	O			O			O
O		X				X	
O	X		O		X		O
			X		X	X	
		X		X			
			O		O	O	
X			X			O	O

49

Combiku

Each horizontal row and vertical column should contain five different shapes, and five different numbers.

Every square will contain one number and one shape, and no combination may be repeated anywhere else in the puzzle; so, for instance, if a square contains a 3 and a star, then no other square containing a 3 will also contain a star, and no other square with a star will also contain a 3.

1 2 3 4 5

	1			
			1	
		3	4	1
1		5		
			3	2

Logi-5

Every row and column of this grid should contain one each of the letters A, B, C, D, and E.

In addition, each of the five shapes (marked by thicker lines) should also contain one each of the letters A, B, C, D, and E.

Can you complete the grid?

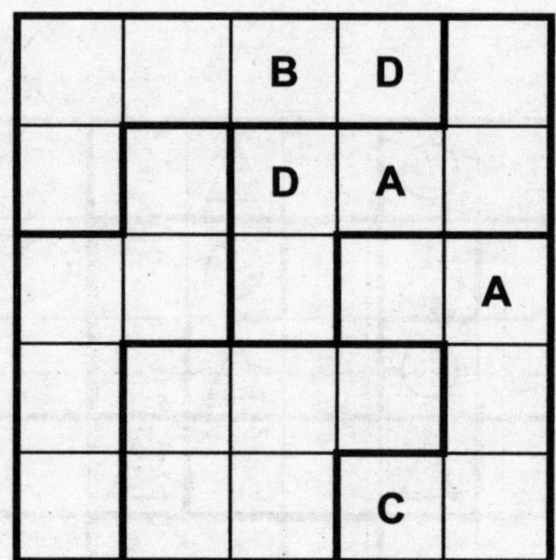

51

Shape Sorter

The grid below is divided into regions of three squares. Some need to contain three different shapes: a circle, a square, and a triangle; others need to contain three identical shapes.

When two squares share a side across a region boundary, the shapes must be different.

○ □ △

	○		△		
			○		○
	○		△		
	△			△	
	□		△		
	△			□	

Chains

Fill each empty circle with one of the numbers 1-6.

Every horizontal row, vertical column, set of six linked circles, and diagonal line of six circles should contain six different numbers.

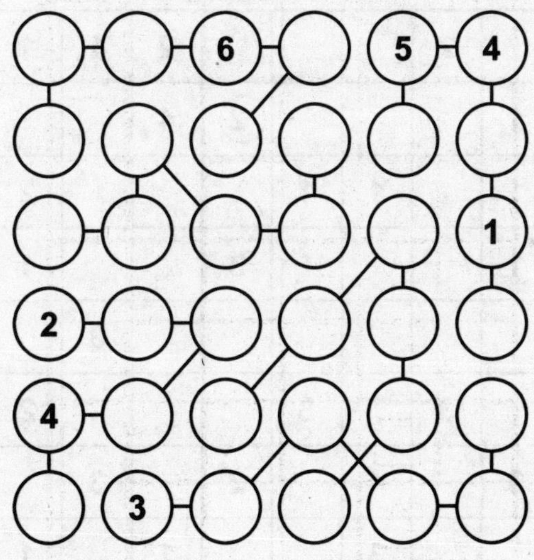

Coin Collecting

In this puzzle, an amateur coin collector has been out with his metal detector, searching for booty. He didn't have time to dig up all the coins he found, so has made a grid map, showing their locations, in the hope that if he loses the map, at least no-one else will understand it... However, he didn't count on YOU coming across the strange grid (as seen here). Will you be able to discover the correct number of coins and their precise locations?

Those squares containing numbers are empty, but where a number appears in a square, it indicates how many coins are located in the squares (up to a maximum of eight) surrounding the numbered one, touching it at any corner or side. There is only one coin in any individual square.

Place a circle into every square containing a coin.

	2				2	1	1
1				2	4		
1		1	1				2
1				3			1
						3	
	3		3				2
3		4		2		3	
		3			1		1

54

Patchwork

Every square should be filled with a letter from A to E, and each heavily outlined set of five squares should contain five different letters. Every row and column must contain two of each letter.

Squares that share a common border may not contain the same letter.

		E	A	C					C
E						B		C	D
D		D			C				C
	D		E			D			
				C		C			B
	D	C			E			B	
E		D	B					E	A
			C	D		C			
A				E		E		C	
	B	A				A			D

55

Slitherlink

Draw a single continuous loop, by connecting the dots. No line may cross the path of another.

The figure inside each set of any four surrounding dots indicates the total number of surrounding lines.

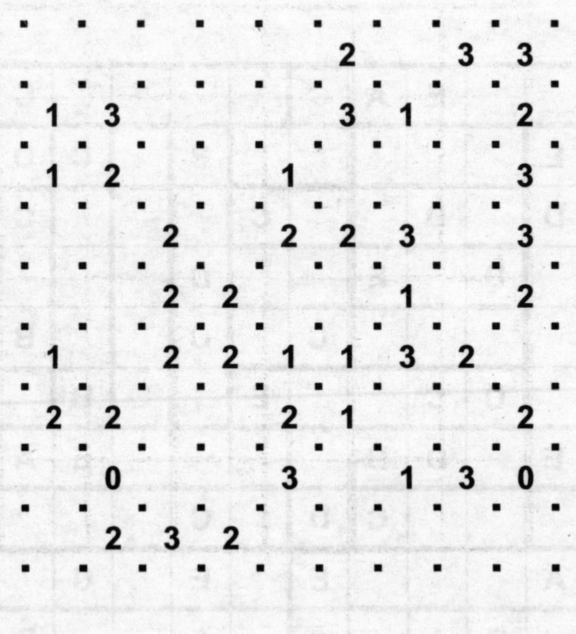

Calcudoku

Each row and column should contain six different numbers from 1 to 6.

The numbers placed in a heavily outlined set of squares may be repeated, but must produce the calculation in the top left corner, using the mathematical symbol provided: multiply (x), divide (/), add (+), and subtract (–).

For example, when multiplied, the numbers 4 and 3 total 12:

12x **4**	**3**

18x	72x		2/		7+
	5/		1–		
		1–	12+	120x	
1–				2/	
16x	12+				3/
			2/		

57

Bridges

Join the circular islands by drawing horizontal or vertical lines to represent bridges, in such a way that the number of bridges connected to each island must match the number on that island. No bridge may cross another, and no more than two bridges can join any pair of islands.

The finished design will allow you to travel from one island to any other island on the map.

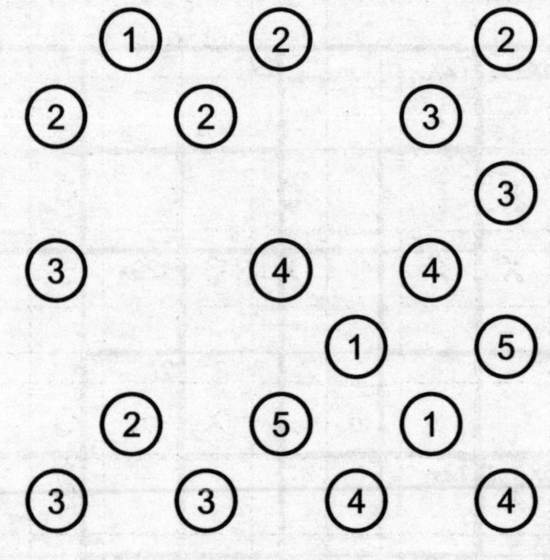

58

No Four in Line

Place either O or X into each empty square, so that no four consecutive squares in a straight line in any direction (horizontally, vertically, or diagonally) contain more than three of the same symbol.

X	O	O	X			O	O	
O					O	X		X
X		X						
	X			O			O	X
X	X	X		X	O			
		O						
					X	X	O	
X	X						O	O
O	O	O			O	O		X

59

Battleships

Can you place the vessels into the diagram? A number to the right or below a row or column refers to the number of occupied squares in that row or column.

Any vessel may be positioned horizontally or vertically, but no part of a vessel touches part of any other vessel, either horizontally, vertically, or diagonally.

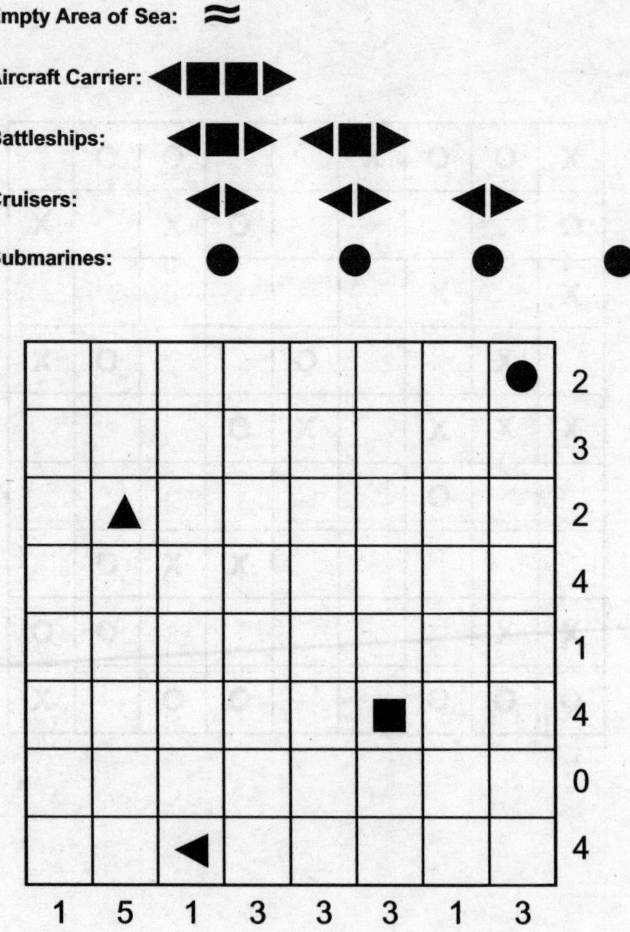

60

Futoshiki

Fill the grid so that every horizontal row and vertical column contains all the numbers 1 to 7.

Any arrows in the grid always point toward a square that contains a lower number.

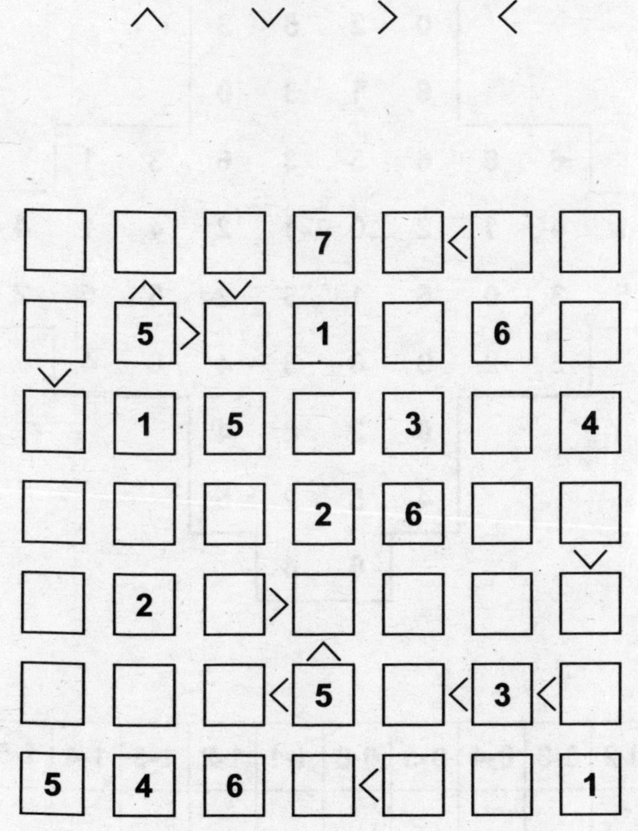

61

Domino Placement

A standard set of 28 dominoes has been laid out as shown. Can you draw in the edges of them all?

The check-box is provided as an aid, so that you can see which dominoes have been located.

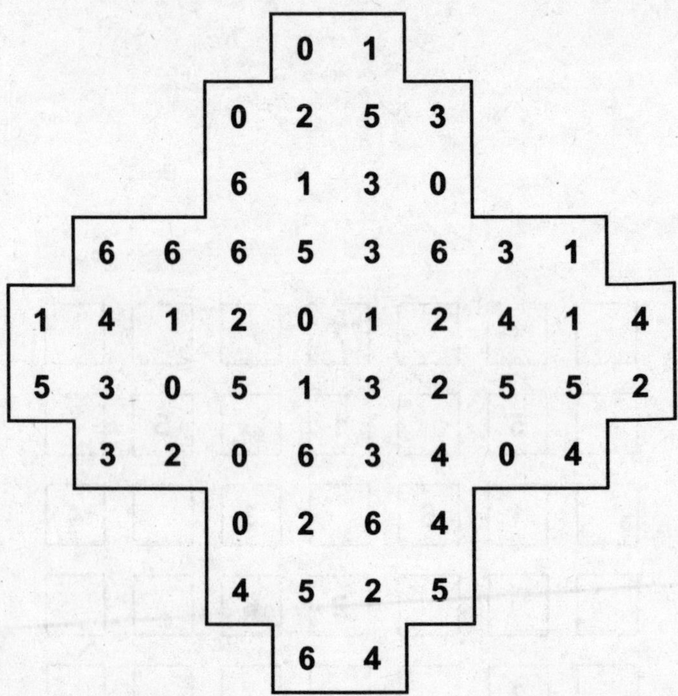

0-0	0-1	0-2	0-3	0-4	0-5	0-6	1-1	1-2	1-3	1-4	1-5	1-6	2-2

2-3	2-4	2-5	2-6	3-3	3-4	3-5	3-6	4-4	4-5	4-6	5-5	5-6	6-6

62

Hidato

Starting at 1 and finishing at 36, track your way from one square to another, either horizontally, vertically, or diagonally, placing consecutive numbers into the empty squares as you go.

18		21	22		26
	17		28		
16			24		31
2	36		34		
1			13	12	11
4		6		9	

63

Sum Total

Fill each empty square so that every row contains ten different numbers from 0 to 9. In columns the numbers may be repeated, but wherever one square touches another, whether horizontally, vertically, or diagonally, the numbers must be different. Some are already in place.

The black squares show the sum total of the numbers in each column.

	2		0		1	9	5		8
9				7	8				3
5	1	3			4	6		0	
		6		1			2		
6	3		8		2		4		0
35	19	23	19	30	15	21	19	18	26

64

Number Link

Working from one square to another, horizontally or vertically (never diagonally), draw single continuous paths to pair up each set of two matching numbers.

No line may cross another, none may travel through any square containing a number, and every square must be visited just once.

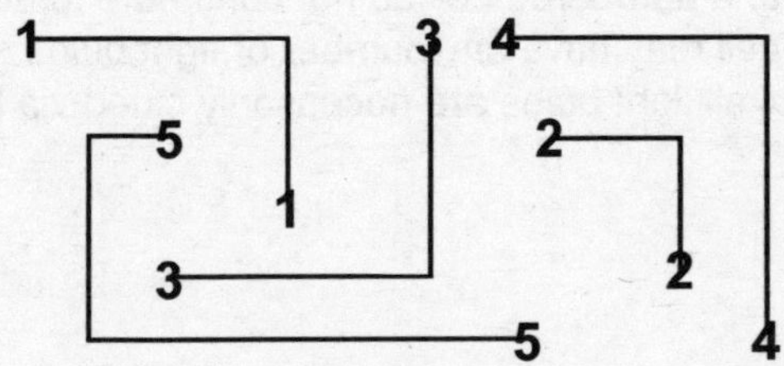

2							2	12
7		7	13	10	12			
9							4	11
14	9							
	13		6	8	6	10	4	
						1		
		5		3		8		
			1					11
14	3							5

Light Up

Place circles (representing light bulbs) in some of the empty squares, in such a way that no two bulbs shine on each other, until every square of the grid is lit up. A bulb sends rays of light horizontally and vertically, illuminating its entire row and column unless its light is blocked by a black cell.

Some black cells contain numbers, indicating how many light bulbs are in adjacent squares either immediately above, below, to the right, or to the left. Bulbs placed diagonally adjacent to a numbered cell do not contribute to the bulb count. An unnumbered black cell may have any number of light bulbs adjacent to it, or none at all, and not all light bulbs are necessarily clued via black squares.

66

Skyscrapers

Place the numbers 1 to 6 into each row and column, one number per square. Each number represents a skyscraper of that many floors.

Arrange the skyscrapers in such a way that the given number outside the grid represents the number of buildings which can be seen from that point, looking only at that number's row or column.

A skyscraper with a lower number of floors cannot hide a higher building, but a one with a higher number of floors always hides any building behind it.

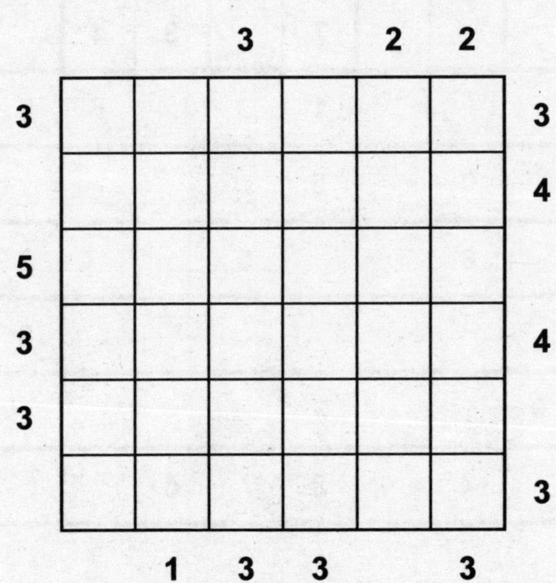

67

Brickwork

Every square should be filled with a number from 1 to 8.
No number may appear twice in any row or column.

Every brick that consists of two squares contains
both an odd number and an even number.

4					5	3	
			7		3	4	
			1	3		6	5
	7		5				
	8			5			2
							8
6			3				
	4		8	7	6		

No Three in Line

Place either O or X into each empty square, so that no three consecutive squares in either a horizontal row or vertical column contain more than two of the same symbol.

There needs to be as many Os as Xs in every row and column.

	O				X		
O					X		
O	X			X		O	
					O		O
	O			X	X		X
X		X	X				
X				O		O	

69

Combiku

Each horizontal row and vertical column should contain five different shapes, and five different numbers.

Every square will contain one number and one shape, and no combination may be repeated anywhere else in the puzzle; so, for instance, if a square contains a 3 and a star, then no other square containing a 3 will also contain a star, and no other square with a star will also contain a 3.

1	2	3	4	5
○	☆	⬡	◇	□

	○	5	3	◇ 4
	□ 1	◇	☆	
	☆			
		○		
		4		☆

70

Logi-6

Every row and column of this grid should contain one each of the letters A, B, C, D, E, and F.

In addition, each of the six shapes (marked by thicker lines) should also contain one each of the letters A, B, C, D, E, and F.

Can you complete the grid?

B	F		C		
		E			
E				D	
	D				
		F			
	A				

71

Shape Sorter

The grid below is divided into regions of three squares. Some need to contain three different shapes: a circle, a square, and a triangle; others need to contain three identical shapes. When two squares share a side across a region boundary, the shapes must be different.

Chains

Fill each empty circle with one of the numbers 1-7.

Every horizontal row, vertical column, set of seven linked circles, and diagonal line of seven circles should contain seven different numbers.

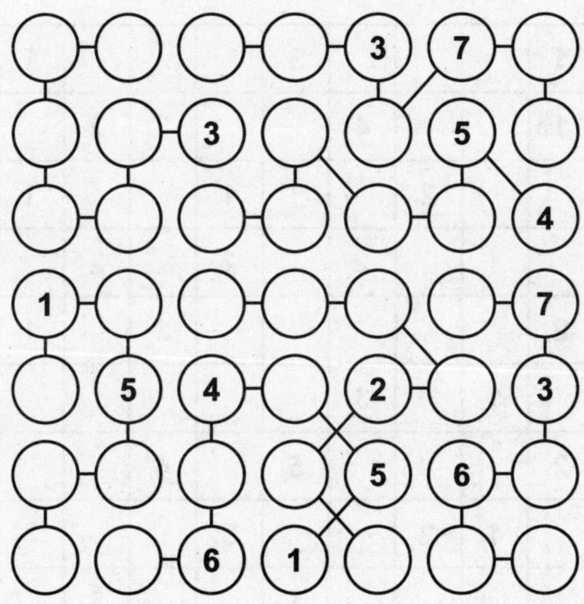

73

Coin Collecting

In this puzzle, an amateur coin collector has been out with his metal detector, searching for booty. He didn't have time to dig up all the coins he found, so has made a grid map, showing their locations, in the hope that if he loses the map, at least no-one else will understand it... However, he didn't count on YOU coming across the strange grid (as seen here). Will you be able to discover the correct number of coins and their precise locations?

Those squares containing numbers are empty, but where a number appears in a square, it indicates how many coins are located in the squares (up to a maximum of eight) surrounding the numbered one, touching it at any corner or side. There is only one coin in any individual square.

Place a circle into every square containing a coin.

1				3				1
1			4				2	
		2		1	1			1
			2		2		2	
2						3		1
	1		3					
2				5		4		
	1	2			3			3
1				1			3	

74

Patchwork

Every square should be filled with a letter from A to E, and each heavily outlined set of five squares should contain five different letters. Every row and column must contain two of each letter.

Squares that share a common border may not contain the same letter.

	A		C	D					
D	B			A	B	C			
			D						E
					B			D	A
C		C				E			
		B				A			C
D	C							A	
E	B				A			C	
		E	B	C			E		

Slitherlink

Draw a single continuous loop, by connecting the dots.
No line may cross the path of another.

The figure inside each set of any four surrounding dots indicates the total number of surrounding lines.

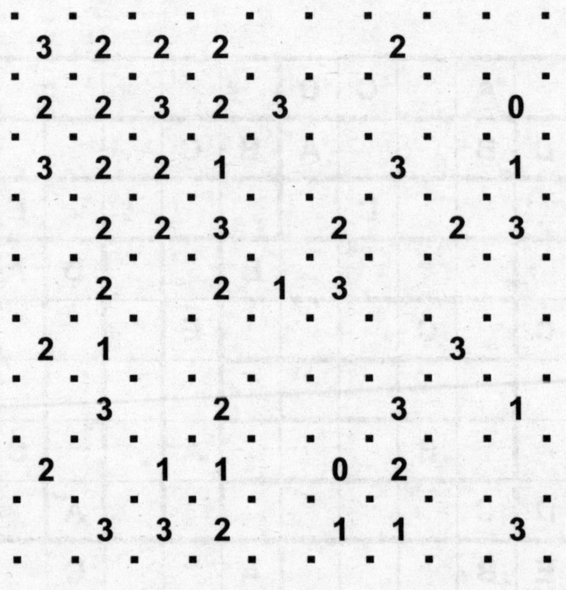

76

Calcudoku

Each row and column should contain six different numbers from 1 to 6.

The numbers placed in a heavily outlined set of squares may be repeated, but must produce the calculation in the top left corner, using the mathematical symbol provided: multiply (x), divide (/), add (+), and subtract (–).

For example, when multiplied, the numbers 4 and 3 total 12:

12x	
4	**3**

15x	8+	240x			
			5/	24x	
9+		1–		3/	
			12+	3/	
360x		3x			1–
			2x		

77

Bridges

Join the circular islands by drawing horizontal or vertical lines to represent bridges, in such a way that the number of bridges connected to each island must match the number on that island. No bridge may cross another, and no more than two bridges can join any pair of islands.

The finished design will allow you to travel from one island to any other island on the map.

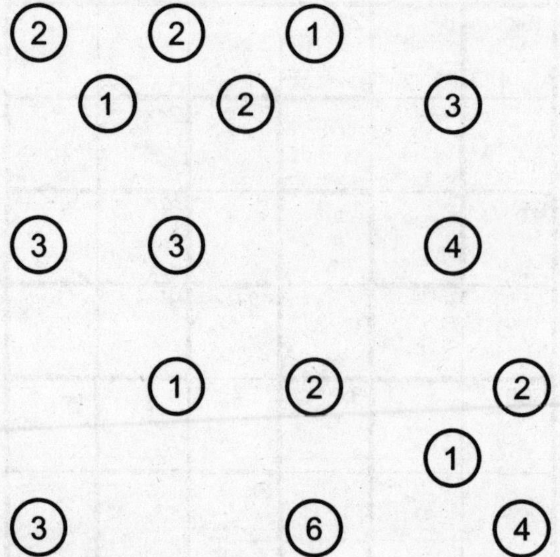

No Four in Line

Place either O or X into each empty square, so that no four consecutive squares in a straight line in any direction (horizontally, vertically, or diagonally) contain more than three of the same symbol.

	O	O				X			X
	X	X					X		X
O	X			O			X	X	
		O			X			X	
X	X		X		X		X	O	
		O			X				O
X				X	O		X		
X	X							O	X
			O		O		O	O	X
X		X			X		X		
	X	O			O		X		

79

Battleships

Can you place the vessels into the diagram? A number to the right or below a row or column refers to the number of occupied squares in that row or column.

Any vessel may be positioned horizontally or vertically, but no part of a vessel touches part of any other vessel, either horizontally, vertically, or diagonally.

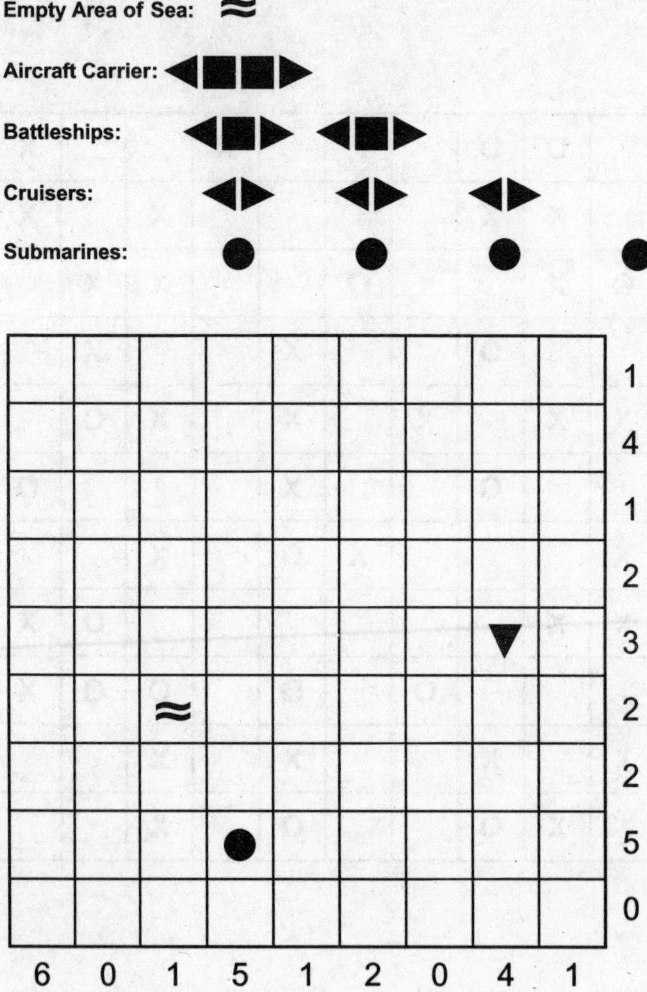

80

Futoshiki

Fill the grid so that every horizontal row and vertical column contains all the numbers 1 to 7.

Any arrows in the grid always point toward a square that contains a lower number.

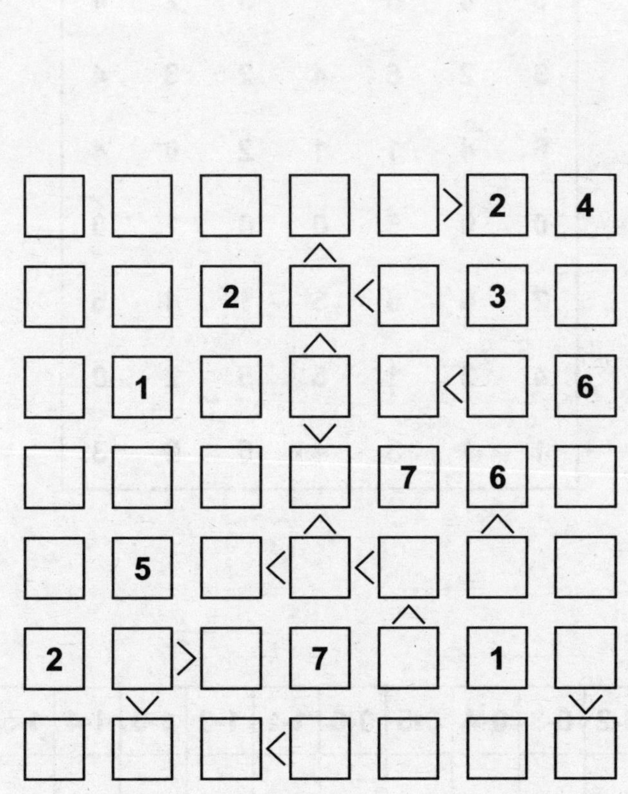

81

Domino Placement

A standard set of 28 dominoes has been laid out as shown. Can you draw in the edges of them all?

The check-box is provided as an aid, so that you can see which dominoes have been located.

6	6	3	2	2	0	5
5	6	3	1	3	2	4
3	2	6	4	2	3	4
6	4	1	1	2	0	4
0	0	5	0	0	1	0
2	6	6	5	1	4	5
4	3	1	5	5	2	0
1	1	3	4	5	6	3

0-0	0-1	0-2	0-3	0-4	0-5	0-6	1-1	1-2	1-3	1-4	1-5	1-6	2-2

2-3	2-4	2-5	2-6	3-3	3-4	3-5	3-6	4-4	4-5	4-6	5-5	5-6	6-6

82

Hidato

Starting at 1 and finishing at 49, track your way from one square to another, either horizontally, vertically, or diagonally, placing consecutive numbers into the empty squares as you go.

12		3	2		42	
13				1		43
14			5			46
8				49		45
		20		35	34	
					31	32
18	25	24		22		

83

Sum Total

Fill each empty square so that every row contains ten different numbers from 0 to 9. In columns the numbers may be repeated, but wherever one square touches another, whether horizontally, vertically, or diagonally, the numbers must be different. Some are already in place.

The black squares show the sum total of the numbers in each column.

8	4			6	9			5	3
		6		3	8		2	7	1
		4	7			3	9		5
		3	5			8			7
9	1	8			0	7			2
8				7	4		6	3	
30	20	23	35	27	30	31	24	27	23

Number Link

Working from one square to another, horizontally or vertically (never diagonally), draw single continuous paths to pair up each set of two matching numbers.

No line may cross another, none may travel through any square containing a number, and every square must be visited just once.

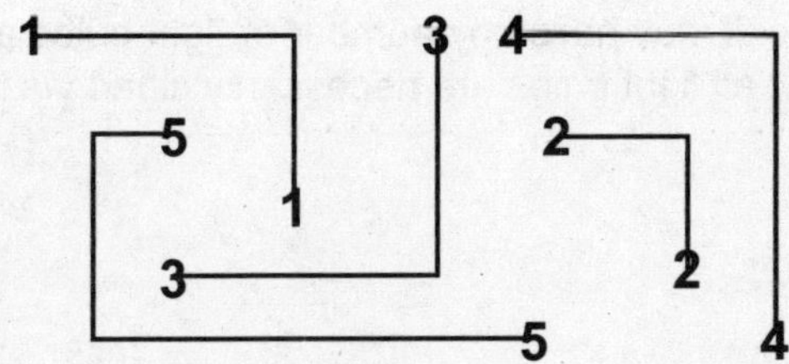

2				16			18		
3				14	5			12	
7						13			
10			2				16	12	18
			3				11		11
		14							13
	7	6			5				1
	10	4	17		1		9		15
4							8	9	
17				6	8	15			

85

Light Up

Place circles (representing light bulbs) in some of the empty squares, in such a way that no two bulbs shine on each other, until every square of the grid is lit up. A bulb sends rays of light horizontally and vertically, illuminating its entire row and column unless its light is blocked by a black cell.

Some black cells contain numbers, indicating how many light bulbs are in adjacent squares either immediately above, below, to the right, or to the left. Bulbs placed diagonally adjacent to a numbered cell do not contribute to the bulb count. An unnumbered black cell may have any number of light bulbs adjacent to it, or none at all, and not all light bulbs are necessarily clued via black squares.

Skyscrapers

Place the numbers 1 to 6 into each row and column, one number per square. Each number represents a skyscraper of that many floors.

Arrange the skyscrapers in such a way that the given number outside the grid represents the number of buildings which can be seen from that point, looking only at that number's row or column.

A skyscraper with a lower number of floors cannot hide a higher building, but one with a higher number of floors always hides any building behind it.

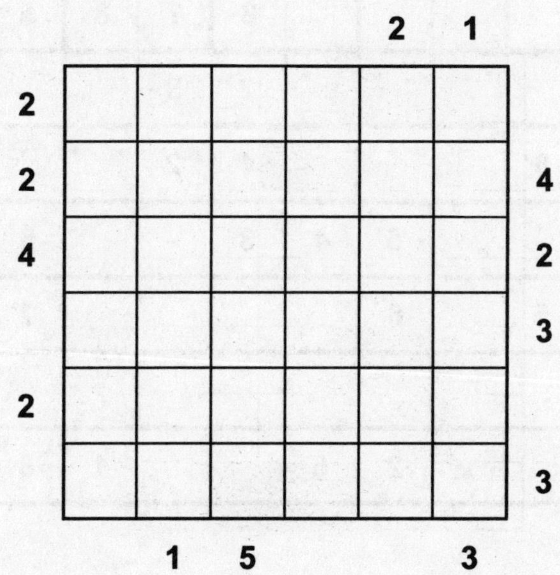

87

Brickwork

Every square should be filled with a number from 1 to 8.
No number may appear twice in any row or column.

Every brick that consists of two squares contains
both an odd number and an even number.

1		8					
				6	7	8	5
				2	5		
6				4	2		
		5	4	3			6
5		6					2
		2	6			1	8

88

No Three in Line

Place either O or X into each empty square, so that no three consecutive squares in either a horizontal row or vertical column contain more than two of the same symbol.

There needs to be as many Os as Xs in every row and column.

					X		X
	O				X	X	
	O		O			O	
							X
		X		O	X		
			X		O		
		O					O
		O	X			O	

89

Combiku

Each horizontal row and vertical column should contain five different shapes, and five different numbers.

Every square will contain one number and one shape, and no combination may be repeated anywhere else in the puzzle; so, for instance, if a square contains a 3 and a star, then no other square containing a 3 will also contain a star, and no other square with a star will also contain a 3.

1	2	3	4	5
○	☆	⬡	◇	□

		○		
	3	☆		◇
	◇	□ 1	5	4
☆	○			⬡
	☆	5		2

90

Logi-6

Every row and column of this grid should contain one each of the letters A, B, C, D, E, and F.

In addition, each of the six shapes (marked by thicker lines) should also contain one each of the letters A, B, C, D, E, and F.

Can you complete the grid?

E	F				
			C	B	
		B	D		F
			E		
D				E	A

91

Shape Sorter

The grid below is divided into regions of three squares. Some need to contain three different shapes: a circle, a square, and a triangle; others need to contain three identical shapes.

When two squares share a side across a region boundary, the shapes must be different.

92

Chains

Fill each empty circle with one of the numbers 1-7.

Every horizontal row, vertical column, set of seven linked circles, and diagonal line of seven circles should contain seven different numbers.

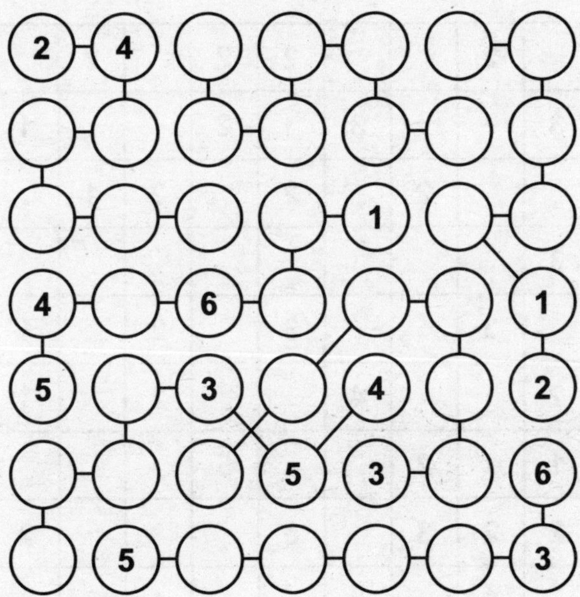

Coin Collecting

In this puzzle, an amateur coin collector has been out with his metal detector, searching for booty. He didn't have time to dig up all the coins he found, so has made a grid map, showing their locations, in the hope that if he loses the map, at least no-one else will understand it... However, he didn't count on YOU coming across the strange grid (as seen here). Will you be able to discover the correct number of coins and their precise locations?

Those squares containing numbers are empty, but where a number appears in a square, it indicates how many coins are located in the squares (up to a maximum of eight) surrounding the numbered one, touching it at any corner or side. There is only one coin in any individual square.

Place a circle into every square containing a coin.

	2			2	2		2	
3			3		2			1
		2		2		2	1	
3								
	3			3		2		1
2			4			2		1
1		2			5			
2	2	3		5				2
	1					4	2	

94

Patchwork

Every square should be filled with a letter from A to E, and each heavily outlined set of five squares should contain five different letters. Every row and column must contain two of each letter.

Squares that share a common border may not contain the same letter.

A		D		D	A		E		C
				B	D		A		
		C	E						
	C			C			B		B
B				E					
	E		D						A
							C		
C							E		D
E	B		D				D		
	D			C	E				E

95

Slitherlink

Draw a single continuous loop, by connecting the dots.
No line may cross the path of another.

The figure inside each set of any four surrounding dots indicates the total number of surrounding lines.

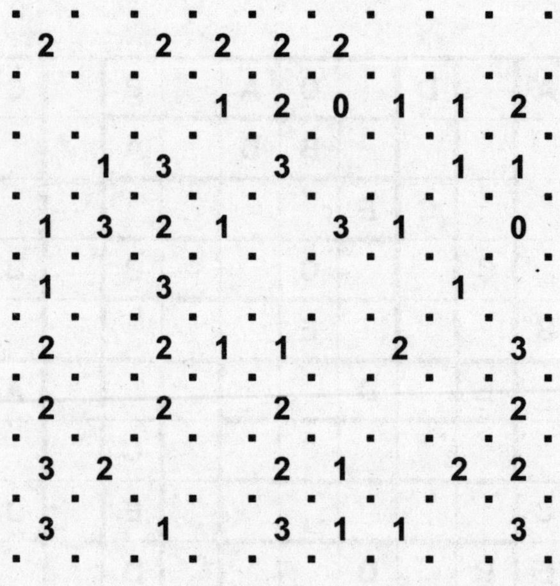

96

Calcudoku

Each row and column should contain six different numbers from 1 to 6.

The numbers placed in a heavily outlined set of squares may be repeated, but must produce the calculation in the top left corner, using the mathematical symbol provided: multiply (x), divide (/), add (+), and subtract (–).

For example, when multiplied, the numbers 4 and 3 total 12:

12x	
4	**3**

3/		10+	20x		
3/	1–			10+	
		7+	3/	2/	10x
30x					
2–	4–	9+		2/	
		4–		3/	

Bridges

Join the circular islands by drawing horizontal or vertical lines to represent bridges, in such a way that the number of bridges connected to each island must match the number on that island. No bridge may cross another, and no more than two bridges can join any pair of islands.

The finished design will allow you to travel from one island to any other island on the map.

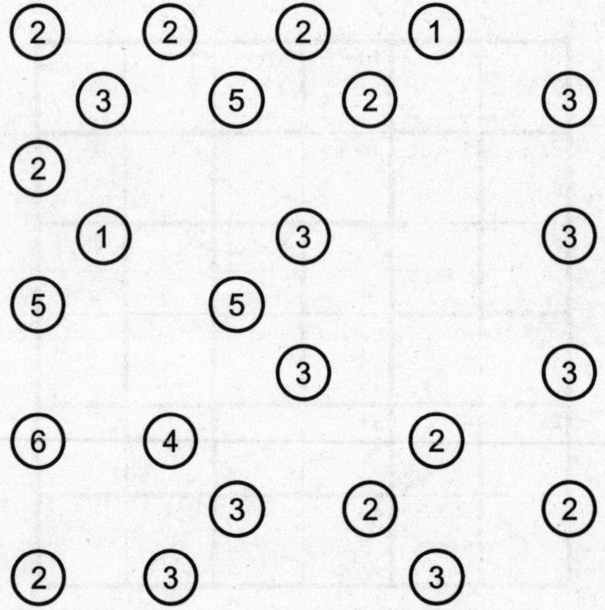

98

No Four in Line

Place either O or X into each empty square, so that no four consecutive squares in a straight line in any direction (horizontally, vertically, or diagonally) contain more than three of the same symbol.

	X	X		O				O	O
X					O		X		
X	X							O	O
X		X				X			
		X			O	O	X		O
				X	O				
		X					X		O
					O	X	X		
X	O		X		X				O
X					X				X
X	X	X		O				O	O

Battleships

Can you place the vessels into the diagram? A number to the right or below a row or column refers to the number of occupied squares in that row or column.

Any vessel may be positioned horizontally or vertically, but no part of a vessel touches part of any other vessel, either horizontally, vertically, or diagonally.

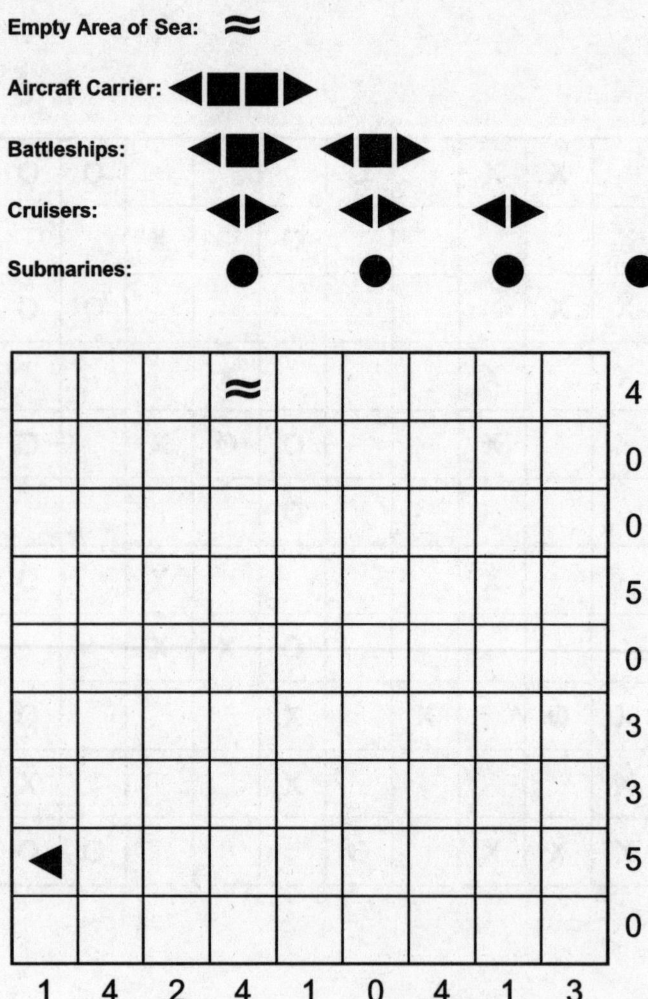

100

Futoshiki

Fill the grid so that every horizontal row and vertical column contains all the numbers 1 to 7.

Any arrows in the grid always point toward a square that contains a lower number.

101

Domino Placement

A standard set of 28 dominoes has been laid out as shown. Can you draw in the edges of them all?

The check-box is provided as an aid, so that you can see which dominoes have been located.

6	3	6	6	0	0	4
5	5	6	0	1	6	1
4	4	0	3	3	2	5
1	5	2	1	0	5	5
5	5	4	1	2	4	2
2	6	0	3	4	2	3
1	3	6	2	6	0	0
3	4	1	2	1	3	4

0-0	0-1	0-2	0-3	0-4	0-5	0-6	1-1	1-2	1-3	1-4	1-5	1-6	2-2

2-3	2-4	2-5	2-6	3-3	3-4	3-5	3-6	4-4	4-5	4-6	5-5	5-6	6-6

102

Hidato

Starting at 1 and finishing at 49, track your way from one square to another, either horizontally, vertically, or diagonally, placing consecutive numbers into the empty squares as you go.

	17	19			26	
15			23	27		30
13			21			31
		1	34			49
	3	9	36		42	
	10			37		
				46		

103

Sum Total

Fill each empty square so that every row contains ten different numbers from 0 to 9. In columns the numbers may be repeated, but wherever one square touches another, whether horizontally, vertically, or diagonally, the numbers must be different. Some are already in place.

The black squares show the sum total of the numbers in each column.

1	4		0	8	6				
	3						8	7	
5						2	0		9
7		0		6	8	9	4		
4		6			3		5		9
	1			9	4			3	8
30	25	26	23	33	34	18	28	23	30

104

Number Link

Working from one square to another, horizontally or vertically (never diagonally), draw single continuous paths to pair up each set of two matching numbers.

No line may cross another, none may travel through any square containing a number, and every square must be visited just once.

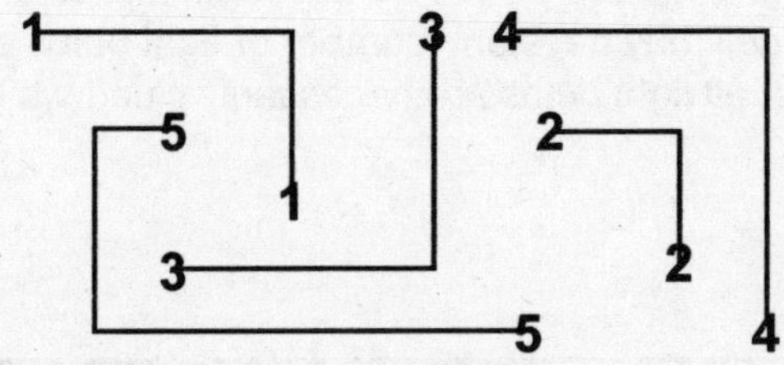

			10		10	13	5	11	9	11
	1									
13					6	7			9	
			4							
8	14							7		
			4							
	2									
		2					3			
				1			12		5	
14	8	6	3							12

Light Up

Place circles (representing light bulbs) in some of the empty squares, in such a way that no two bulbs shine on each other, until every square of the grid is lit up. A bulb sends rays of light horizontally and vertically, illuminating its entire row and column unless its light is blocked by a black cell.

Some black cells contain numbers, indicating how many light bulbs are in adjacent squares either immediately above, below, to the right, or to the left. Bulbs placed diagonally adjacent to a numbered cell do not contribute to the bulb count. An unnumbered black cell may have any number of light bulbs adjacent to it, or none at all, and not all light bulbs are necessarily clued via black squares.

			1				
2							
0	0			0			
		2		3		2	

Skyscrapers

Place the numbers 1 to 6 into each row and column, one number per square. Each number represents a skyscraper of that many floors.

Arrange the skyscrapers in such a way that the given number outside the grid represents the number of buildings which can be seen from that point, looking only at that number's row or column.

A skyscraper with a lower number of floors cannot hide a higher building, but one with a higher number of floors always hides any building behind it.

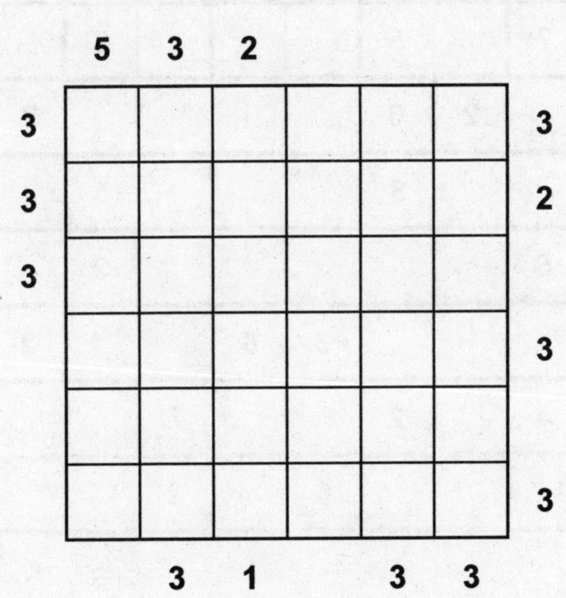

Brickwork

Every square should be filled with a number from 1 to 8.
No number may appear twice in any row or column.

Every brick that consists of two squares contains both an odd number and an even number.

					1		
7		5				6	
	2	6					7
		8				5	
6						2	
			3	8			2
4		2			7		
			8		2		

108

No Three in Line

Place either O or X into each empty square, so that no three consecutive squares in either a horizontal row or vertical column contain more than two of the same symbol.

There needs to be as many Os as Xs in every row and column.

X							X
		X					
	X		O				
					O		
	X	X			O		X
O						O	
	X		X				
					X		

109

Combiku

Each horizontal row and vertical column should contain five different shapes, and five different numbers.

Every square will contain one number and one shape, and no combination may be repeated anywhere else in the puzzle; so, for instance, if a square contains a 3 and a star, then no other square containing a 3 will also contain a star, and no other square with a star will also contain a 3.

1	2	3	4	5
○	☆	⬡	◇	□

	4			
◇ 5	⬡		□	
	○	□ 5		4
2			☆	
□	☆	3		

110

Logi-6

Every row and column of this grid should contain one each of the letters A, B, C, D, E, and F.

In addition, each of the six shapes (marked by thicker lines) should also contain one each of the letters A, B, C, D, E, and F.

Can you complete the grid?

A			D		
			C	A	
				E	
D				F	
		E			
			F		

111

Shape Sorter

The grid below is divided into regions of three squares. Some need to contain three different shapes: a circle, a square, and a triangle; others need to contain three identical shapes.

When two squares share a side across a region boundary, the shapes must be different.

○ □ △

		○		○			
□			□				
				△		□	
	△				○		
□			△				△
	□					△	
			□			□	
				△	○		□
	□		○				

112

Chains

Fill each empty circle with one of the numbers 1-7.

Every horizontal row, vertical column, set of seven linked circles, and diagonal line of seven circles should contain seven different numbers.

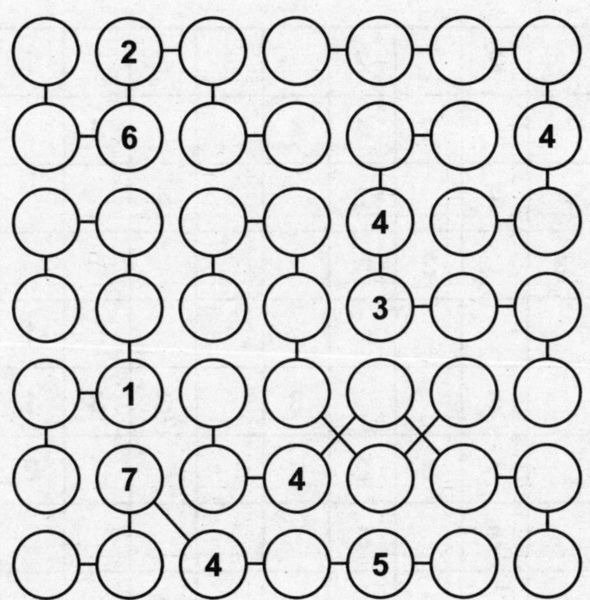

Coin Collecting

In this puzzle, an amateur coin collector has been out with his metal detector, searching for booty. He didn't have time to dig up all the coins he found, so has made a grid map, showing their locations, in the hope that if he loses the map, at least no-one else will understand it... However, he didn't count on YOU coming across the strange grid (as seen here). Will you be able to discover the correct number of coins and their precise locations?

Those squares containing numbers are empty, but where a number appears in a square, it indicates how many coins are located in the squares (up to a maximum of eight) surrounding the numbered one, touching it at any corner or side. There is only one coin in any individual square.

Place a circle into every square containing a coin.

	2		2		3	3		1
		2	4	4			4	
	2		2			4		
3		3						
								1
	5			3		3	3	1
		3	2					2
	5		3					
2		3				4	2	

114

Patchwork

Every square should be filled with a letter from A to E, and each heavily outlined set of five squares should contain five different letters. Every row and column must contain two of each letter.

Squares that share a common border may not contain the same letter.

A			D					C	
					A				
	C	B		B		E			
	D	E						C	
			A				B		B
			B			C		A	
A		C						B	
	E					D			E
			D			B			
	A				B				D

115

Slitherlink

Draw a single continuous loop, by connecting the dots.
No line may cross the path of another.

The figure inside each set of any four surrounding dots indicates the total number of surrounding lines.

3		1	1	2			1	2	3
			0			3	3		
1	2	3				1			2
2	1	2		3	2	1	2		
		3			0	2		1	
1						3		1	
2			3			3		3	1
			2	3		3			
2			0		1	2		2	
	3	2	1		3	2			2
	3		2	2		2		3	

Calcudoku

Each row and column should contain seven different numbers from 1 to 7.

The numbers placed in a heavily outlined set of squares may be repeated, but must produce the calculation in the top left corner, using the mathematical symbol provided: multiply (x), divide (/), add (+), and subtract (–).

For example, when multiplied, the numbers 4 and 3 total 12:

12x	
4	**3**

3/		28x	24x	1–		12+
11+	30x			1–		
			11+	5/		
	5–	1–		2/	14+	
126x						15+
	3–	3–		4+		
		5+		11+		

117

Bridges

Join the circular islands by drawing horizontal or vertical lines to represent bridges, in such a way that the number of bridges connected to each island must match the number on that island. No bridge may cross another, and no more than two bridges can join any pair of islands.

The finished design will allow you to travel from one island to any other island on the map.

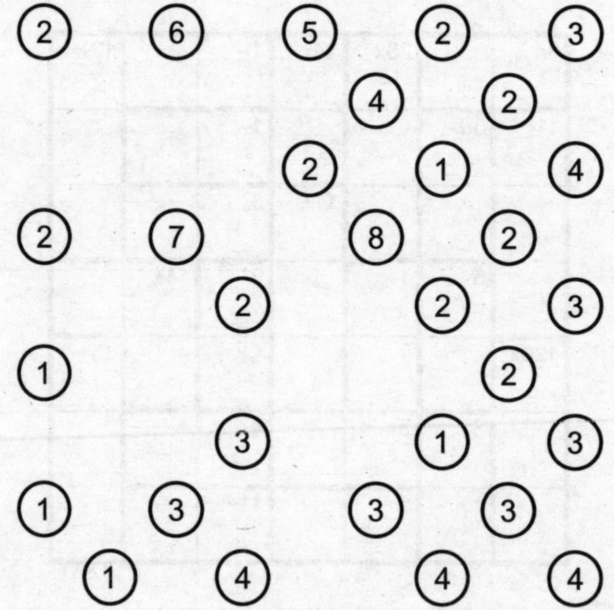

118

No Four in Line

Place either O or X into each empty square, so that no four consecutive squares in a straight line in any direction (horizontally, vertically, or diagonally) contain more than three of the same symbol.

	X	X			O		O	X	O
X		O				O			X
	O	O	O						X
X		X			X	O	X	O	
	O							X	X
						O			
	X	X			O			O	O
O			X			X			
X		X		X		O			
X	O	X	O			O			O
O	O	O		O	X			X	

119

Battleships

Can you place the vessels into the diagram? A number to the right or below a row or column refers to the number of occupied squares in that row or column.

Any vessel may be positioned horizontally or vertically, but no part of a vessel touches part of any other vessel, either horizontally, vertically, or diagonally.

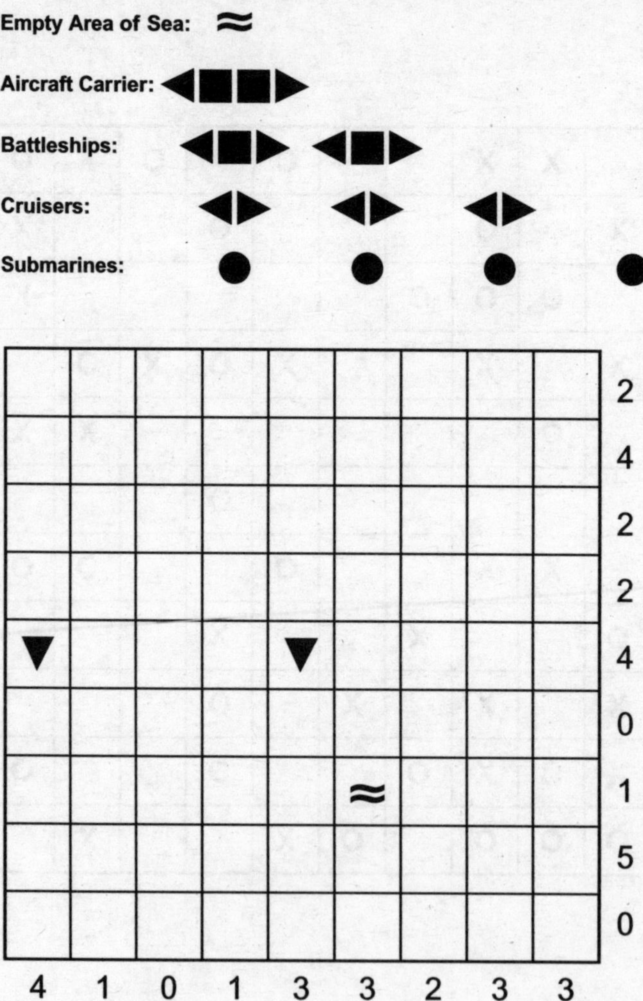

120

Futoshiki

Fill the grid so that every horizontal row and vertical column contains all the numbers 1 to 7.

Any arrows in the grid always point toward a square that contains a lower number.

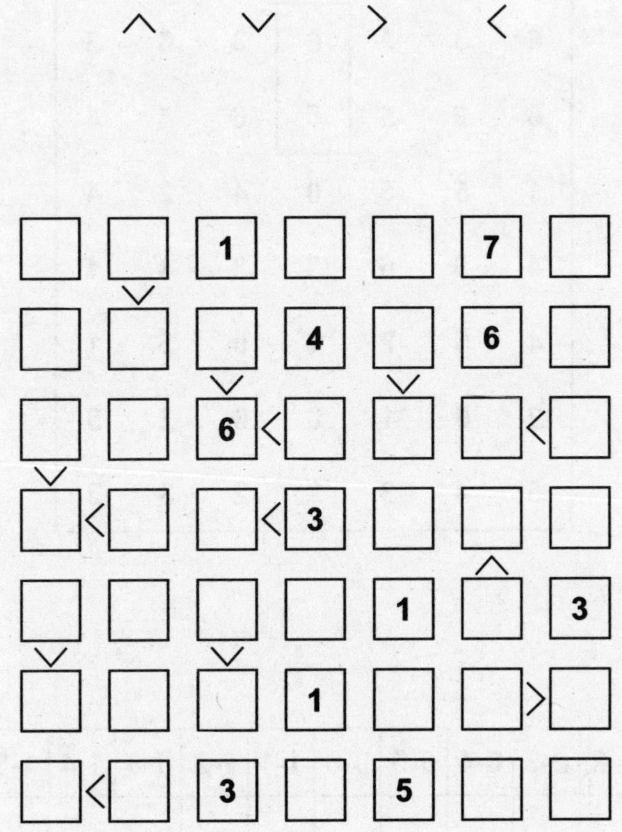

121

Domino Placement

A standard set of 28 dominoes has been laid out as shown. Can you draw in the edges of them all?

The check-box is provided as an aid, so that you can see which dominoes have been located.

2	0	0	1	1	6	0
6	3	1	6	3	6	3
6	2	5	5	6	4	4
1	5	5	0	4	2	4
4	0	6	3	3	4	1
4	5	2	1	0	5	1
2	6	1	0	0	2	5
5	4	3	2	2	3	3

0-0	0-1	0-2	0-3	0-4	0-5	0-6	1-1	1-2	1-3	1-4	1-5	1-6	2-2

2-3	2-4	2-5	2-6	3-3	3-4	3-5	3-6	4-4	4-5	4-6	5-5	5-6	6-6
												✓	

122

Hidato

Starting at 1 and finishing at 49, track your way from one square to another, either horizontally, vertically, or diagonally, placing consecutive numbers into the empty squares as you go.

					48	49
10		6				46
12	15					
			1	35	33	
	39	40				
	18		24	25	30	
19		22	23			28

Sum Total

Fill each empty square so that every row contains ten different numbers from 0 to 9. In columns the numbers may be repeated, but wherever one square touches another, whether horizontally, vertically, or diagonally, the numbers must be different. Some are already in place.

The black squares show the sum total of the numbers in each column.

			1		6		8		
9		5	7			2			0
8		3			5			1	2
		1	0		9	7	5	8	
	9	2	6		5	8		3	0
1				0			4		9
35	28	19	25	19	35	23	31	31	24

124

Number Link

Working from one square to another, horizontally or vertically (never diagonally), draw single continuous paths to pair up each set of two matching numbers.

No line may cross another, none may travel through any square containing a number, and every square must be visited just once.

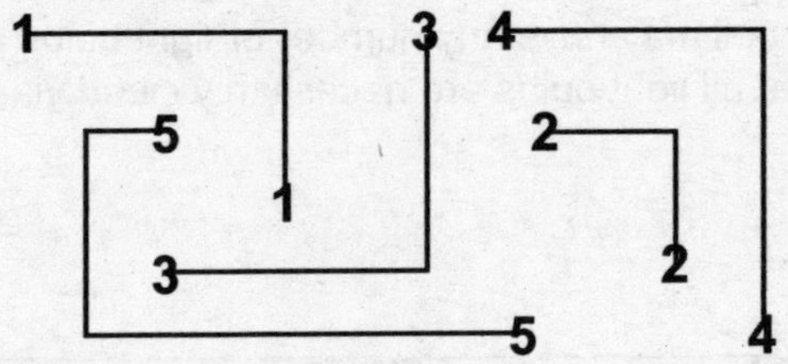

				2						
2										
		4			7	12		13		
	11		3			7		4		6
			8							
					8					
								13		
6			1	5						
			3			10				12
	9			5				1		10
		11								9

125

Light Up

Place circles (representing light bulbs) in some of the empty squares, in such a way that no two bulbs shine on each other, until every square of the grid is lit up. A bulb sends rays of light horizontally and vertically, illuminating its entire row and column unless its light is blocked by a black cell.

Some black cells contain numbers, indicating how many light bulbs are in adjacent squares either immediately above, below, to the right, or to the left. Bulbs placed diagonally adjacent to a numbered cell do not contribute to the bulb count. An unnumbered black cell may have any number of light bulbs adjacent to it, or none at all, and not all light bulbs are necessarily clued via black squares.

126

Skyscrapers

Place the numbers 1 to 6 into each row and column, one number per square. Each number represents a skyscraper of that many floors.

Arrange the skyscrapers in such a way that the given number outside the grid represents the number of buildings which can be seen from that point, looking only at that number's row or column.

A skyscraper with a lower number of floors cannot hide a higher building, but one with a higher number of floors always hides any building behind it.

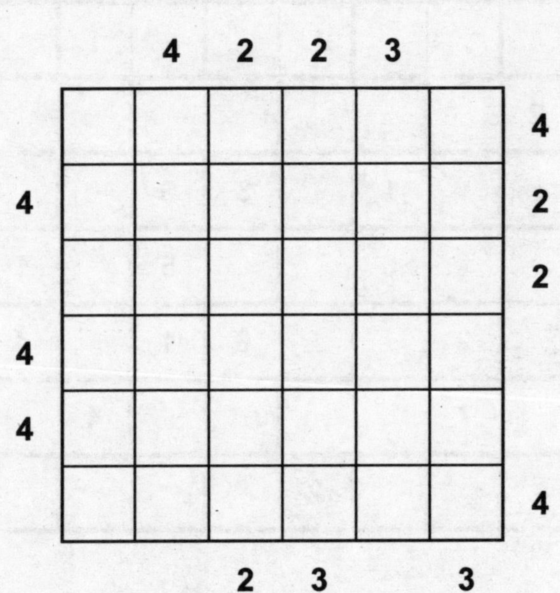

127

Brickwork

Every square should be filled with a number from 1 to 8.
No number may appear twice in any row or column.

Every brick that consists of two squares contains
both an odd number and an even number.

1			8			5	
4						1	
2							
		1		3	6		
		6			5		1
	2			6	1		4
	7					4	
			2				

128

No Three in Line

Place either O or X into each empty square, so that no three consecutive squares in either a horizontal row or vertical column contain more than two of the same symbol.

There needs to be as many Os as Xs in every row and column.

O							
O	O				O		
				O			
O	O		O				
					X		O
	O		X				
				O		X	
	X		X		X		

Combiku

Each horizontal row and vertical column should contain five different shapes, and five different numbers.

Every square will contain one number and one shape, and no combination may be repeated anywhere else in the puzzle; so, for instance, if a square contains a 3 and a star, then no other square containing a 3 will also contain a star, and no other square with a star will also contain a 3.

1 2 3 4 5

4				
		1		4
		4		5
		2		
			1	

130

Logi-7

Every row and column of this grid should contain one each of the letters A, B, C, D, E, F, and G.

In addition, each of the seven shapes (marked by thicker lines) should also contain one each of the letters A, B, C, D, E, F, and G.

Can you complete the grid?

			E			
	A			B		
	D	F			C	
			G		A	
G	E					

131

Shape Sorter

The grid below is divided into regions of three squares. Some need to contain three different shapes: a circle, a square, and a triangle; others need to contain three identical shapes.

When two squares share a side across a region boundary, the shapes must be different.

○ □ △

○			□	△				
	○					△		○
○					○			□
						○		
	□	○		□			□	○
	○			○	△			
		△					△	□
	△		□		○			

Chains

Fill each empty circle with one of the numbers 1-8.

Every horizontal row, vertical column, set of eight linked circles, and diagonal line of eight circles should contain eight different numbers.

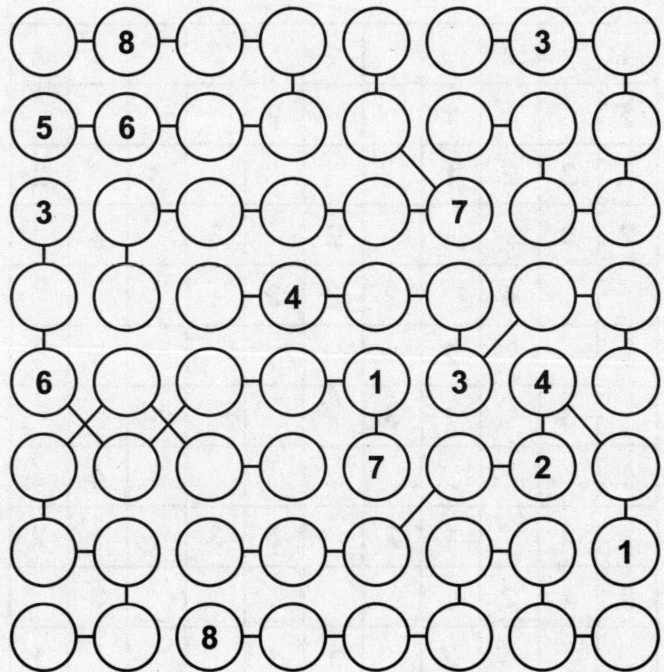

133

Coin Collecting

In this puzzle, an amateur coin collector has been out with his metal detector, searching for booty. He didn't have time to dig up all the coins he found, so has made a grid map, showing their locations, in the hope that if he loses the map, at least no-one else will understand it... However, he didn't count on YOU coming across the strange grid (as seen here). Will you be able to discover the correct number of coins and their precise locations?

Those squares containing numbers are empty, but where a number appears in a square, it indicates how many coins are located in the squares (up to a maximum of eight) surrounding the numbered one, touching it at any corner or side. There is only one coin in any individual square.

Place a circle into every square containing a coin.

1		2			1		2		3	2
1			1			2				
	2	2	1					3		2
2	3				2		3		4	
		4		2	2	3				
			2			3			6	4
	3		1	3						
1								3	4	
			1	2		5	3			2
2	4	2							3	
			2		1	1				1

134

Patchwork

Every square should be filled with a letter from A to F, and each heavily outlined set of six squares should contain six different letters. Every row and column must contain two of each letter.

Squares that share a common border may not contain the same letter.

		D	F			A				F	
E		E	A			F					F
	B						C			D	
		C		E		F		A			B
D			C		E			F		B	E
F		F				E				E	
	F						D				
E				F	B		E				
			A		D				C		
D		A			B				E		F
F	D	E					C	B			
		D	E		C						C

135

Slitherlink

Draw a single continuous loop, by connecting the dots. No line may cross the path of another.

The figure inside each set of any four surrounding dots indicates the total number of surrounding lines.

2			3		3	3		1	3
1	2	1	2					3	
	2	1	1		2	3			
		2		1		2	2	3	3
	2	1	3	3			3		2
2	3								
3		1	1		2				2
		3		3	2				
	2				1	1	3	2	1
2	3	1		3		0		1	2
2		0					3	1	2
3				1	1	3		2	2

136

Calcudoku

Each row and column should contain eight different numbers from 1 to 8.

The numbers placed in a heavily outlined set of squares may be repeated, but must produce the calculation in the top left corner, using the mathematical symbol provided: multiply (x), divide (/), add (+), and subtract (–).

For example, when multiplied, the numbers 4 and 3 total 12:

12x	
4	3

3/		14+	2/		48X	3–	8/
5–	3–			5+			
		7/			8+	2–	
12+		480x		28x		14+	
						12+	
2–		12x		35x		2x	
18x	28x	4/	48x				2–
			1–		7+		

137

Bridges

Join the circular islands by drawing horizontal or vertical lines to represent bridges, in such a way that the number of bridges connected to each island must match the number on that island. No bridge may cross another, and no more than two bridges can join any pair of islands.

The finished design will allow you to travel from one island to any other island on the map.

		1			3			4	
									1
2			1			4		4	
									3
								1	
						5			5
4			3		2				
2			2			2			1

138

No Four in Line

Place either O or X into each empty square, so that no four consecutive squares in a straight line in any direction (horizontally, vertically, or diagonally) contain more than three of the same symbol.

<table>
<tr><td></td><td>O</td><td></td><td></td><td></td><td></td><td></td><td>O</td><td></td><td>O</td></tr>
<tr><td>O</td><td></td><td>X</td><td></td><td></td><td></td><td>O</td><td></td><td>O</td><td>O</td></tr>
<tr><td>O</td><td>X</td><td></td><td>X</td><td></td><td></td><td></td><td>O</td><td></td><td>O</td></tr>
<tr><td></td><td>X</td><td>X</td><td></td><td></td><td></td><td></td><td></td><td></td><td></td></tr>
<tr><td>O</td><td>X</td><td></td><td>O</td><td></td><td>O</td><td></td><td>O</td><td></td><td></td></tr>
<tr><td></td><td></td><td></td><td></td><td></td><td></td><td></td><td>O</td><td>O</td><td></td></tr>
<tr><td></td><td>O</td><td></td><td>O</td><td></td><td>O</td><td></td><td></td><td>X</td><td>X</td></tr>
<tr><td>X</td><td>X</td><td></td><td></td><td></td><td></td><td>O</td><td>X</td><td></td><td>X</td></tr>
<tr><td></td><td></td><td></td><td></td><td></td><td>O</td><td></td><td></td><td></td><td>O</td></tr>
<tr><td></td><td></td><td>O</td><td></td><td></td><td></td><td></td><td></td><td></td><td>O</td></tr>
<tr><td>X</td><td>X</td><td></td><td></td><td></td><td></td><td></td><td>X</td><td></td><td></td></tr>
<tr><td></td><td>O</td><td>O</td><td></td><td></td><td>O</td><td></td><td>O</td><td></td><td>O</td></tr>
<tr><td>X</td><td>X</td><td></td><td>O</td><td></td><td></td><td></td><td>X</td><td>X</td><td>X</td></tr>
</table>

139

Battleships

Can you place the vessels into the diagram? A number to the right or below a row or column refers to the number of occupied squares in that row or column.

Any vessel may be positioned horizontally or vertically, but no part of a vessel touches part of any other vessel, either horizontally, vertically, or diagonally.

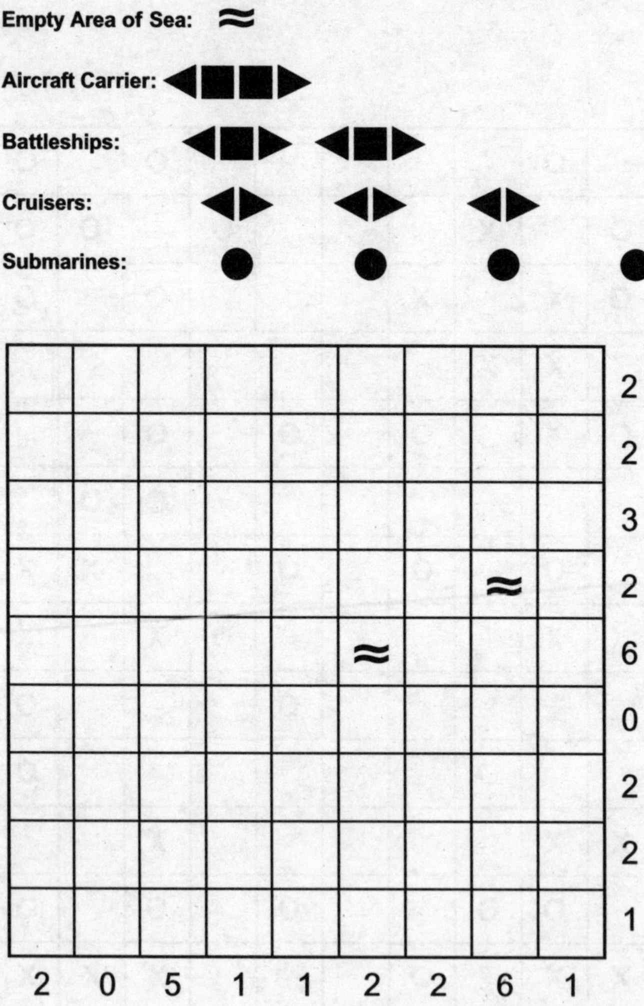

140

Futoshiki

Fill the grid so that every horizontal row and vertical column contains all the numbers 1 to 8.

Any arrows in the grid always point toward a square that contains a lower number.

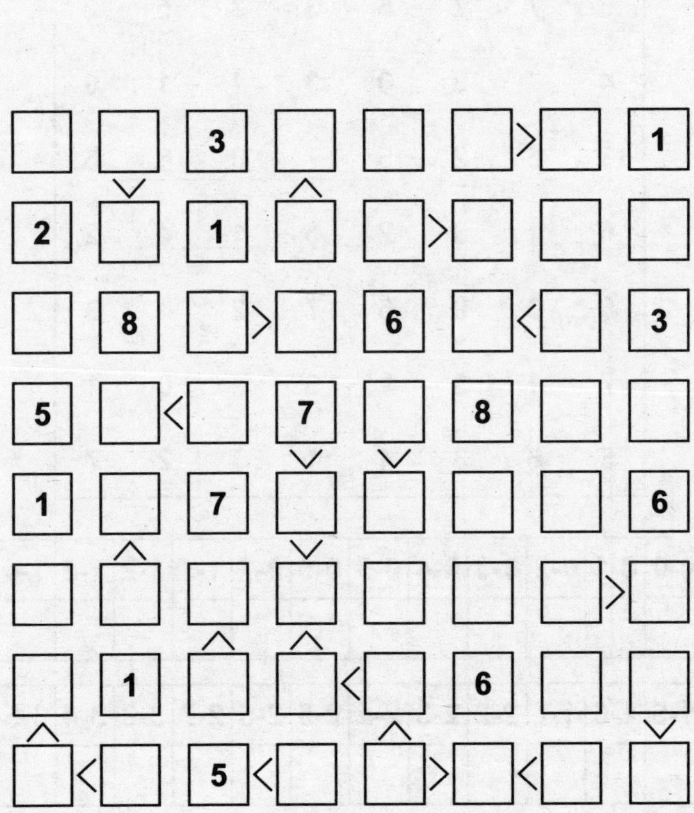

Domino Placement

A set of 36 dominoes has been laid out as shown.
Can you draw in the edges of them all?

The check-box is provided as an aid, so that you can see which dominoes have been located.

4	0	4	4	5	6	7	4
0	2	2	1	4	0	5	1
6	7	7	5	3	3	5	2
4	7	3	0	3	1	1	0
3	6	2	5	7	0	6	5
6	1	3	2	5	1	4	2
5	0	0	6	7	2	4	3
7	1	5	2	6	7	0	1
6	6	3	4	1	3	2	7

0-0	0-1	0-2	0-3	0-4	0-5	0-6	0-7	1-1	1-2	1-3	1-4

1-5	1-6	1-7	2-2	2-3	2-4	2-5	2-6	2-7	3-3	3-4	3-5

3-6	3-7	4-4	4-5	4-6	4-7	5-5	5-6	5-7	6-6	6-7	7-7

Hidato

Starting at 1 and finishing at 64, track your way from one square to another, either horizontally, vertically, or diagonally, placing consecutive numbers into the empty squares as you go.

		22	30			33	1
	25	29		31			34
26				16	18		35
52							36
	51			39	13	37	
60		58				12	
64				44	47		
62			45		10	9	

Sum Total

Fill each empty square so that every row contains ten different numbers from 0 to 9. In columns the numbers may be repeated, but wherever one square touches another, whether horizontally, vertically, or diagonally, the numbers must be different. Some are already in place.

The black squares show the sum total of the numbers in each column.

8		2	1		7				
	5				1		4	8	3
8						5		0	
2		9			7		4	6	1
5	1			4			8	9	0
	6		8			3			1
29	26	29	33	22	31	22	28	27	23

144

Number Link

Working from one square to another, horizontally or vertically (never diagonally), draw single continuous paths to pair up each set of two matching numbers.

No line may cross another, none may travel through any square containing a number, and every square must be visited just once.

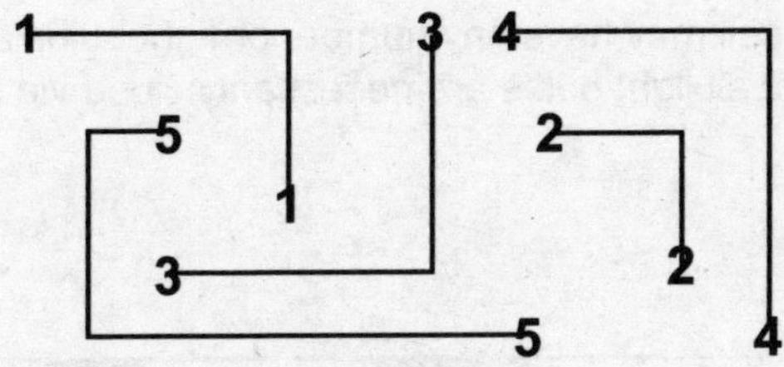

	6		4	8						
										8
6	4	15		14			5			11
15										14
				13	10	11		1		1
		9	3			10				5
	9		7							
	7		2					2	12	
	3									
12			13							

145

Light Up

Place circles (representing light bulbs) in some of the empty squares, in such a way that no two bulbs shine on each other, until every square of the grid is lit up. A bulb sends rays of light horizontally and vertically, illuminating its entire row and column unless its light is blocked by a black cell.

Some black cells contain numbers, indicating how many light bulbs are in adjacent squares either immediately above, below, to the right, or to the left. Bulbs placed diagonally adjacent to a numbered cell do not contribute to the bulb count. An unnumbered black cell may have any number of light bulbs adjacent to it, or none at all, and not all light bulbs are necessarily clued via black squares.

				■			1	
■		2		0		1		
								■
						1		
		■						
	2		0					
■				■	0			■
		3						
	2					1		

146

Skyscrapers

Place the numbers 1 to 7 into each row and column, one number per square. Each number represents a skyscraper of that many floors.

Arrange the skyscrapers in such a way that the given number outside the grid represents the number of buildings which can be seen from that point, looking only at that number's row or column.

A skyscraper with a lower number of floors cannot hide a higher building, but one with a higher number of floors always hides any building behind it.

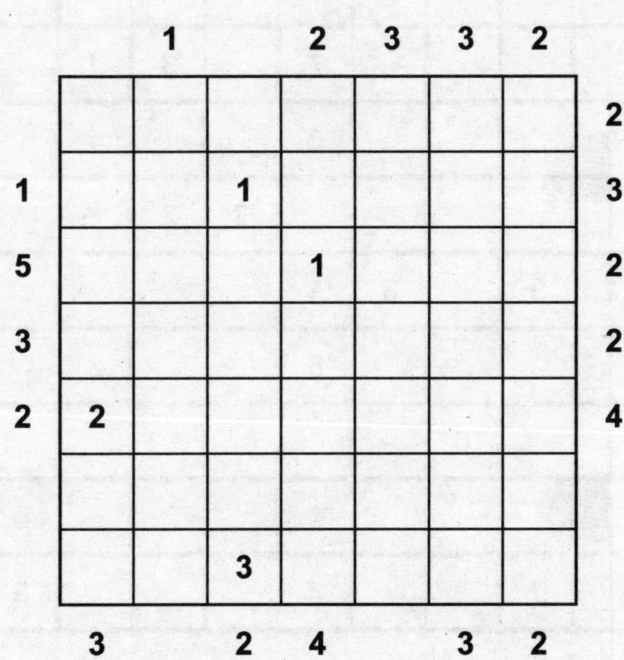

147

Brickwork

Every square should be filled with a number from 1 to 9.
No number may appear twice in any row or column.

Every brick that consists of two squares contains both an odd number and an even number.

		5		6		9	8	
				7		3	1	
9				3			4	
					3	2		
2	9		8	1				
				8			3	
		6						
								4
	7			4				5

No Three in Line

Place either O or X into each empty square, so that no three consecutive squares in either a horizontal row or vertical column contain more than two of the same symbol.
There needs to be as many Os as Xs in every row and column.

O			X			X			
			X			O			
		X			O			X	
O	O					O			O
X									X
				O		X			
X	X								X
					X				
		O	O			O			
			X		O	O			

Combiku

Each horizontal row and vertical column should contain five different shapes, and five different numbers.

Every square will contain one number and one shape, and no combination may be repeated anywhere else in the puzzle; so, for instance, if a square contains a 3 and a star, then no other square containing a 3 will also contain a star, and no other square with a star will also contain a 3.

1 2 3 4 5

			4	
		4		
				3
	5	3		
		1		

150

Logi-7

Every row and column of this grid should contain one each of the letters A, B, C, D, E, F, and G.

In addition, each of the seven shapes (marked by thicker lines) should also contain one each of the letters A, B, C, D, E, F, and G.

Can you complete the grid?

		B		D	A	
		E		G		
						G
D	G					
		A			C	
			F			

151

Shape Sorter

The grid below is divided into regions of three squares. Some need to contain three different shapes: a circle, a square, and a triangle; others need to contain three identical shapes.

When two squares share a side across a region boundary, the shapes must be different.

○ □ △

	□				□			△
	○			□				
	□	○		○		△		
△								
						□		△
		□		△				○
	△					○		
○		△			○			
						△		○

152

Chains

Fill each empty circle with one of the numbers 1-8.

Every horizontal row, vertical column, set of eight linked circles, and diagonal line of eight circles should contain eight different numbers.

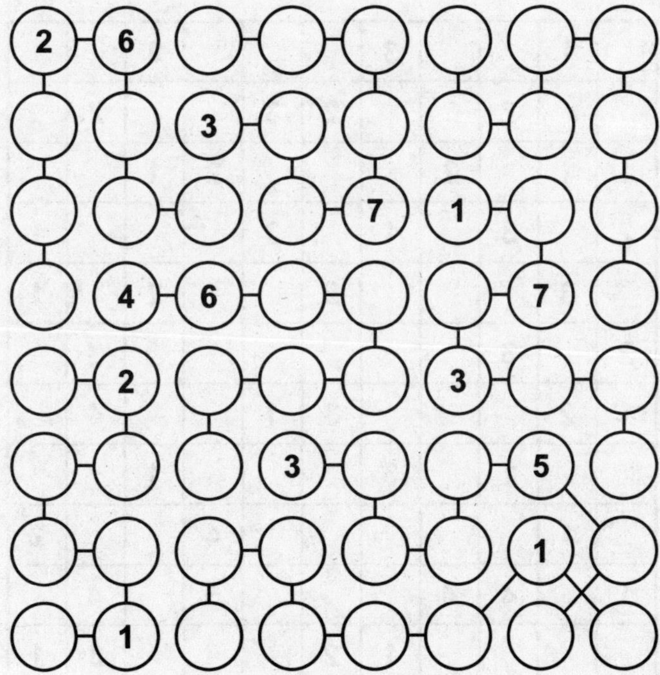

153

Coin Collecting

In this puzzle, an amateur coin collector has been out with his metal detector, searching for booty. He didn't have time to dig up all the coins he found, so has made a grid map, showing their locations, in the hope that if he loses the map, at least no-one else will understand it... However, he didn't count on YOU coming across the strange grid (as seen here). Will you be able to discover the correct number of coins and their precise locations?

Those squares containing numbers are empty, but where a number appears in a square, it indicates how many coins are located in the squares (up to a maximum of eight) surrounding the numbered one, touching it at any corner or side. There is only one coin in any individual square.

Place a circle into every square containing a coin.

	1			3				3		
		2			2	3			2	
1	1		2				2	1		
2		3		1		3				1
	3				2			2		1
2		3							3	
	2				3	1			4	
		1		3				1		
	1						4			2
1		4	4				5		4	
				1	2				3	1

154

Patchwork

Every square should be filled with a letter from A to F, and each heavily outlined set of six squares should contain six different letters. Every row and column must contain two of each letter.

Squares that share a common border may not contain the same letter.

	D	E	C		B			D	E	A	
					C		F			C	E
B	F		A					F			
					D	F					
			A		B						C
		B			D		E		F		
			B	E	A					B	
	D						F		B		
D				B	A					A	
		E		A		E		B	A	C	
	B		F				B	F			
	F			C			E				D

155

Slitherlink

Draw a single continuous loop, by connecting the dots. No line may cross the path of another.

The figure inside each set of any four surrounding dots indicates the total number of surrounding lines.

3	3	3	2			1	1	2	2
1		2		3	2				
2	1		2	2	0	2		2	3
			2		1		1	1	3
	2	1							
3		1	2			2	2		0
3				1		1	3		2
2			2		3	1			3
	3						3	2	2
2	2		3	1			2	2	
		1	3	0				2	2
2	1			2			2	1	3

156

Calcudoku

Each row and column should contain eight different numbers from 1 to 8.

The numbers placed in a heavily outlined set of squares may be repeated, but must produce the calculation in the top left corner, using the mathematical symbol provided: multiply (x), divide (/), add (+), and subtract (–).

For example, when multiplied, the numbers 4 and 3 total 12:

12x 4	3

5–	7/		5–		17+	2/	
	3/		20x			21x	
15x		14x				11+	6/
14x	9+	480x					
		7+		4–	2/	14+	
24x		30x				16+	
	192x	19+		9+		10x	
			18x				

157

Bridges

Join the circular islands by drawing horizontal or vertical lines to represent bridges, in such a way that the number of bridges connected to each island must match the number on that island. No bridge may cross another, and no more than two bridges can join any pair of islands.

The finished design will allow you to travel from one island to any other island on the map.

1		4		2		2		2
							1	
	3	6			1			2
							3	
								2
		4			2			
	4		3				4	
		1		4		3		2
	2			3			1	

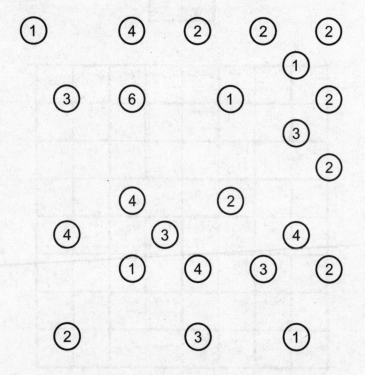

158

No Four in Line

Place either O or X into each empty square, so that no four consecutive squares in a straight line in any direction (horizontally, vertically, or diagonally) contain more than three of the same symbol.

	X	X	O				X	X	X
O	X					X	O	X	O
X									
	X				O			X	
	X	X							O
X	X			O			X		
						O			
	O					O			
O						O		O	X
				X			O		X
	O							O	
	O	O				X			
	O	O	O			X	X	O	

159

Battleships

Can you place the vessels into the diagram? A number to the right or below a row or column refers to the number of occupied squares in that row or column.

Any vessel may be positioned horizontally or vertically, but no part of a vessel touches part of any other vessel, either horizontally, vertically, or diagonally.

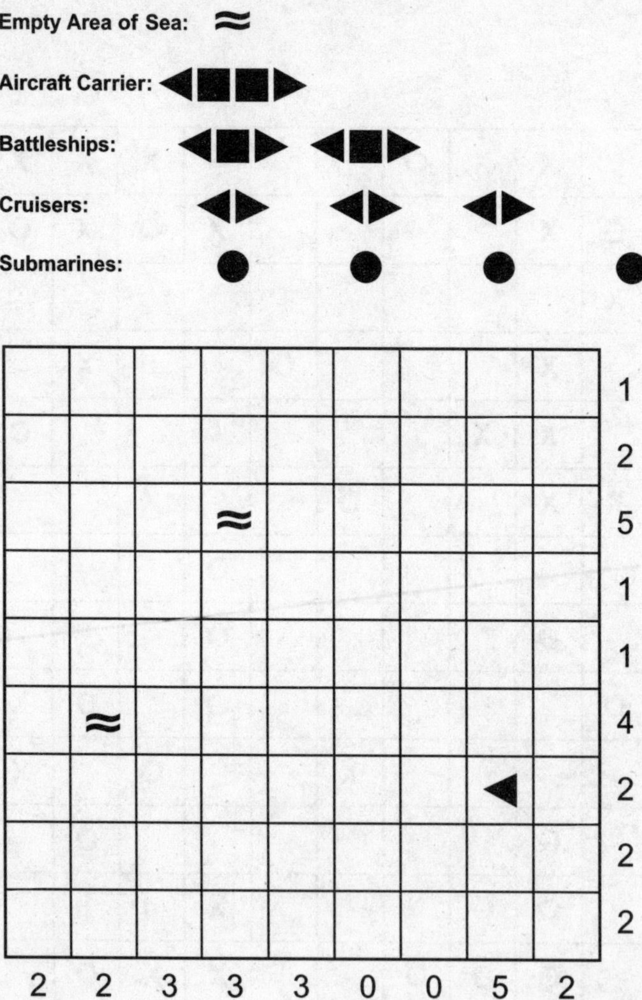

160

Futoshiki

Fill the grid so that every horizontal row and vertical column contains all the numbers 1 to 8.

Any arrows in the grid always point toward a square that contains a lower number.

∧ ∨ > <

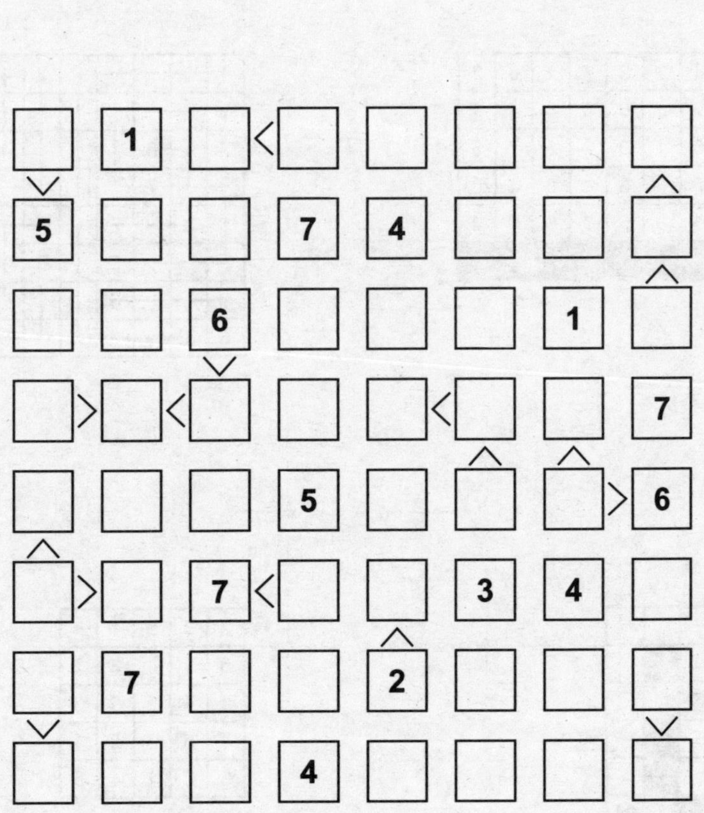

1

				1	3				
			2	0	0	4			
			2	0	2	2			
	0	6	1	5	6	3	2	1	
6	4	5	4	5	2	3	3	5	6
1	1	0	1	0	3	1	4	3	6
	6	5	0	5	5	4	6	3	
			6	1	5	3			
			2	0	2	4			
				4	4				

2

33	34	35	8	11	12
32	36	7	9	10	13
31	5	6	2	15	14
30	29	4	3	1	16
28	25	23	21	20	17
26	27	24	22	18	19

3

5	8	0	4	3	9	7	1	6	2
2	6	7	9	5	0	3	8	4	1
8	4	3	0	1	9	2	6	7	5
7	9	2	8	6	3	4	5	1	0
2	6	3	1	0	5	7	8	9	4
24	33	15	22	15	26	23	28	27	12

4

1					2	4	9
7		5				4	9
		7		1			
	3		3				
			5		8		
			6			10	
6	10					8	2

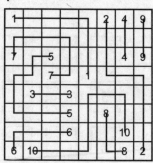

5

1	1	●			
●	2			0	
	●	2	●		
				0	
				0	
	1	●	1		●

6

2	3	5	1	4
5	1	4	3	2
1	4	2	5	3
4	5	3	2	1
3	2	1	4	5

7

2	5	3	4	1	6
6	2	5	3	4	1
3	4	2	1	6	5
1	3	4	6	5	2
5	6	1	2	3	4
4	1	6	5	2	3

8

X	O	O	X	X	O	O	X
O	O	X	O	X	O	X	X
O	X	X	O	O	X	X	O
X	O	O	X	X	O	O	X
O	X	X	O	O	X	X	O
O	O	X	O	X	X	O	X
X	X	O	X	O	O	X	O
X	X	O	X	O	X	O	O

9

○ 4	◇ 1	⬡ 2	☆ 3
☆ 1	⬡ 4	◇ 3	○ 2
◇ 2	○ 3	☆ 4	⬡ 1
⬡ 3	☆ 2	○ 1	◇ 4

10

D	B	E	C	A
B	E	A	D	C
C	A	D	B	E
E	D	C	A	B
A	C	B	E	D

11

□	○	△	□	△	□
△	□	○	□	△	□
□	○	△	□	△	□
△	△	□	○	○	△
○	△	○	△	○	□
○	○	△	○	□	○

12

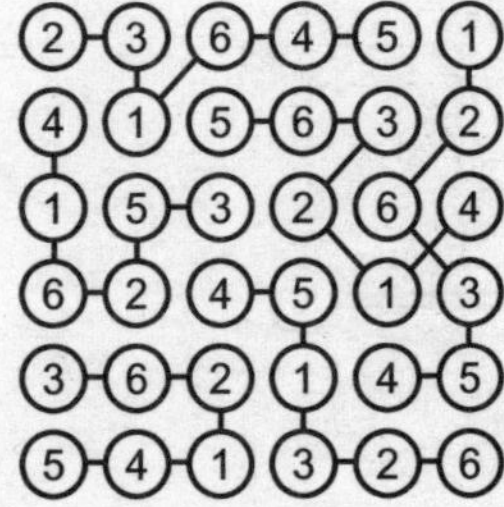

13

●	3	●		1	●	3	2
●		1			5	●	●
●	4		2	●	●	●	3
4	●	●	3		4		1
●	●	●	4		●	2	
3	5	●	●	2	1		●
●	3	3		2			2
1		●			●	2	●

14

C	D	A	B	C	D	A	B
D	A	B	C	B	A	D	C
B	C	A	D	A	C	B	D
C	A	D	B	D	B	C	A
B	D	C	A	C	D	A	B
A	B	D	C	A	C	B	D
D	C	B	A	D	B	C	A
A	B	C	D	B	A	D	C

15

2	1	2		1	3	3	2	
2	1	1	2		1	2	1	2
2			1	2	1			2
		1	2	3	2	2		2
		2	2	1	2		1	1
3	2	2		2		3	1	1
	2	2		3	1	2		
	3	3	2	2	3	3		1
	1	2	2	1		0	2	

16

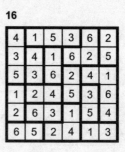

4	1	5	3	6	2
3	4	1	6	2	5
5	3	6	2	4	1
1	2	4	5	3	6
2	6	3	1	5	4
6	5	2	4	1	3

17

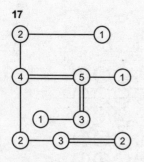

18

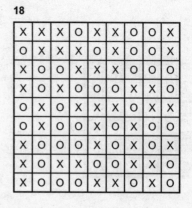

X	X	X	O	X	X	O	O	X
O	X	X	X	O	X	O	O	X
X	O	O	X	X	X	O	O	O
X	O	X	O	O	O	X	X	O
O	X	O	X	X	X	O	X	X
O	X	O	O	X	O	X	O	O
X	O	O	O	X	O	X	O	X
X	O	X	X	O	O	X	X	O
X	O	O	O	X	X	O	X	O

19

	◀	▶					▲
				▲			■
	▲			▼			■
	■						▼
	▼						
			●		▲		●
▲					■		
▼			●		▼		●

20

5	2	3	6	4	1
4	3	1	5	2	6
6	4	2	1	3	5
1	6	4	2	5	3
2	1	5	3	6	4
3	5	6	4	1	2

21

				6	5				
			3	5	3	3			
			0	5	1	4			
	1	1	0	1	2	0	6	6	
0	0	2	6	1	5	1	0	2	2
4	4	3	1	1	2	3	6	5	4
	4	6	2	2	3	2	3	4	
			5	5	0	5			
			4	3	0	4			
				6	6				

22

1	31	30	29	5	6
32	2	3	4	28	7
35	33	11	9	8	27
34	36	12	10	20	26
15	14	13	19	25	21
16	17	18	24	23	22

23

2	9	4	3	8	1	6	7	5	0
8	0	1	9	2	7	5	3	4	6
2	4	8	0	6	3	1	7	9	5
0	9	3	7	1	8	5	6	4	2
6	4	1	9	5	2	0	3	8	7
18	26	17	28	22	21	17	26	30	20

24

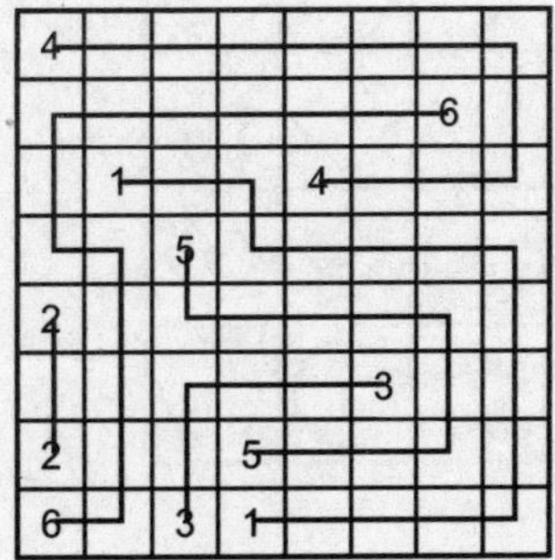

25

1	●				
		●			1
1					●
●		1	●		
		0			0
0				●	1

26

1	2	3	5	4
3	1	4	2	5
5	4	2	3	1
4	3	5	1	2
2	5	1	4	3

27

2	3	5	4	1	6
6	2	1	3	4	5
3	4	2	5	6	1
5	1	4	6	3	2
4	5	6	1	2	3
1	6	3	2	5	4

28

O	O	X	O	X	O	X	X
X	X	O	O	X	O	X	O
O	O	X	X	O	X	O	X
O	O	X	X	O	O	X	X
X	X	O	O	X	X	O	O
O	O	X	X	O	O	X	X
X	X	O	X	O	X	O	O
X	X	O	O	X	X	O	O

29

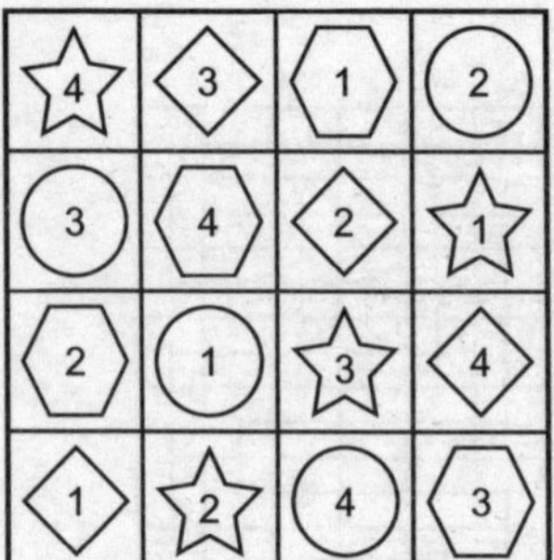

30

E	D	B	A	C
D	C	A	B	E
A	B	E	C	D
B	E	C	D	A
C	A	D	E	B

31

□	□	□	△	△	△
△	○	△	○	□	□
△	△	□	○	△	□
□	○	△	○	△	△
□	○	△	□	□	□
□	○	△	○	○	○

32

3	6	2	1	5	4
4	5	1	6	3	2
2	3	4	5	6	1
5	1	6	2	4	3
6	2	3	4	1	5
1	4	5	3	2	6

33

●	2	●	2	●			●
		2		1	1	2	2
●	2	●		1			●
2			2		●		1
●	3	●	3			2	
3	●	4	●	●		●	1
●	4		●	3		3	3
●	●		1			●	●

34

C	A	E	D	B	A	D	C	E	B
E	C	D	B	A	B	C	A	D	E
D	A	E	A	D	C	B	E	B	C
C	E	B	E	C	A	D	B	A	D
E	B	D	B	E	C	A	D	C	A
B	C	B	A	C	D	E	A	D	E
A	D	C	D	A	E	B	C	E	B
D	B	A	C	E	D	C	E	B	A
A	D	C	E	B	E	A	B	C	D
B	E	A	C	D	B	E	D	A	C

35

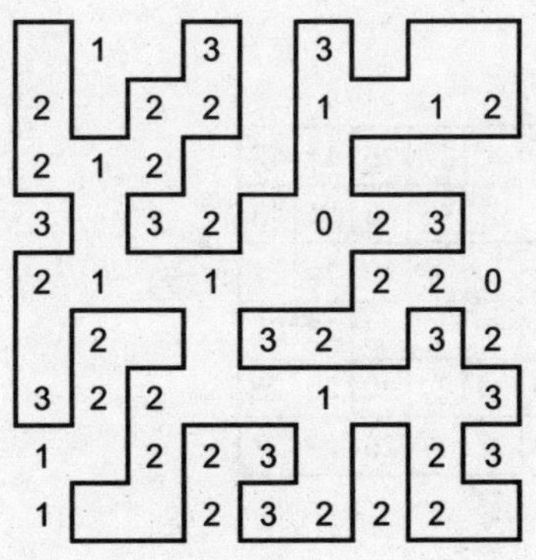

36

2	1	4	6	3	5
6	4	2	1	5	3
1	2	3	5	4	6
5	3	1	4	6	2
3	6	5	2	1	4
4	5	6	3	2	1

37

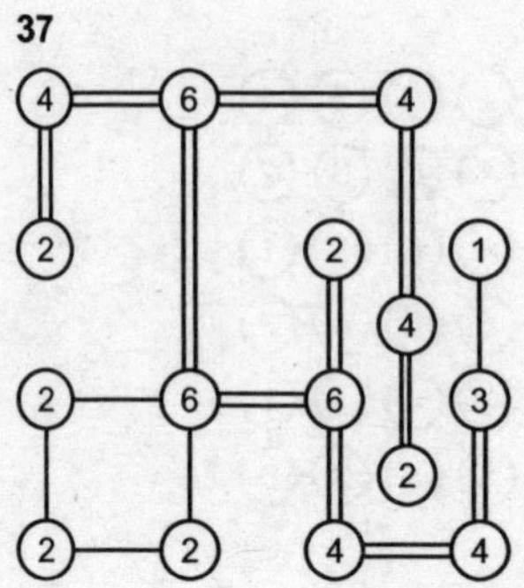

38

X	O	X	O	X	X	X	O	O
O	O	O	X	O	O	O	X	X
X	X	O	O	O	X	O	O	O
X	X	O	X	X	X	O	X	X
O	X	X	O	O	X	X	O	O
O	O	X	O	O	O	X	O	O
O	X	O	O	O	X	O	O	X
X	X	O	X	X	X	O	X	X
X	X	X	O	X	X	O	X	X

39

	◀	▶			▲		●
					■		
	◀	▶			▼		●
	◀	▶					●
					▲		
					■		
◀	■	■	▶		▼		●

40

5	2	1	7	4	6	3
7	1	3	6	5	4	2
4	7	2	5	6	3	1
6	4	5	3	2	1	7
3	6	4	2	1	7	5
1	5	7	4	3	2	6
2	3	6	1	7	5	4

41

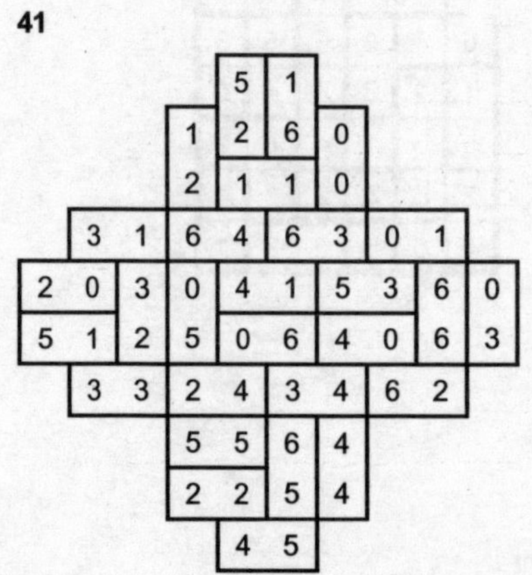

42

3	4	17	15	14	12
5	2	16	18	11	13
1	6	7	10	19	21
35	8	9	23	22	20
36	34	24	30	29	28
33	32	31	25	26	27

43

6	0	5	7	4	9	8	1	3	2
1	3	4	9	8	5	2	6	7	0
0	2	1	5	7	6	4	8	9	3
5	6	9	0	3	1	7	2	4	8
4	8	1	7	5	2	3	9	6	0
16	19	20	28	27	23	24	26	29	13

44

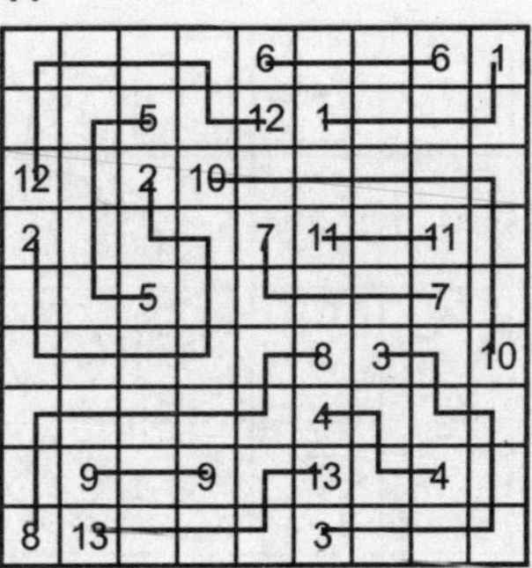

45

	●					
1			0		●	
●						
	0			0		1
0		●		0	1	●
			●			
●	1				●	1

46

5	4	1	2	3
1	3	2	5	4
4	2	3	1	5
3	1	5	4	2
2	5	4	3	1

47

4	5	2	1	3	6
2	6	1	3	4	5
1	4	5	2	6	3
3	1	6	4	5	2
5	2	3	6	1	4
6	3	4	5	2	1

48

X	X	O	O	X	O	O	X
X	O	O	X	O	X	X	O
O	O	X	X	O	O	X	X
O	X	X	O	X	X	O	O
X	O	O	X	O	X	X	O
O	O	X	O	X	O	X	X
O	X	X	O	X	O	O	X
X	X	O	X	O	X	O	O

49

2	1	4	5	3
3	4	2	1	5
5	2	3	4	1
1	3	5	2	4
4	5	1	3	2

50

E	A	B	D	C
C	E	D	A	B
D	C	E	B	A
A	B	C	E	D
B	D	A	C	E

51

△	○	□	△	○	□
○	□	△	○	△	○
○	○	△	△	□	△
□	△	○	□	△	○
△	○	△	○	○	□
○	□	○	△	○	△
□	△	□	○	□	○

52

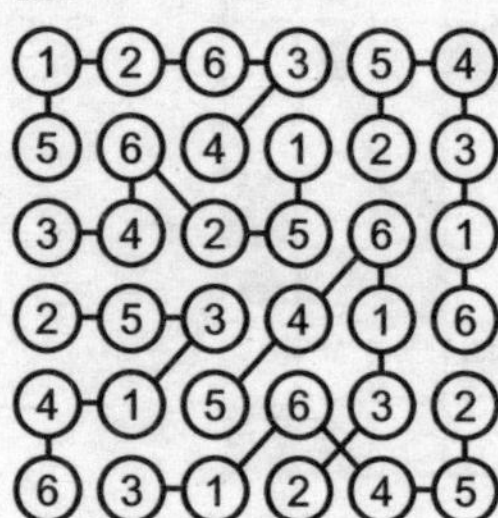

53

●	2	●		●	2	1	1
1				2	4	●	
1		1	1	●		●	2
1	●			3	●		1
		●			●	3	
	3	●	3			●	2
3	●	4	●	2	●	3	●
●	●	3			1		1

54

D	B	E	A	C	E	D	B	A	C
E	A	B	C	E	D	B	A	C	D
D	E	D	B	A	C	E	B	A	C
B	D	C	E	B	A	D	C	E	A
A	E	A	D	C	B	C	E	D	B
C	D	C	A	B	E	A	D	B	E
E	C	D	B	A	D	B	C	E	A
B	A	E	C	D	B	C	A	D	E
A	C	B	D	E	A	E	D	C	B
C	B	A	E	D	C	A	E	B	D

55

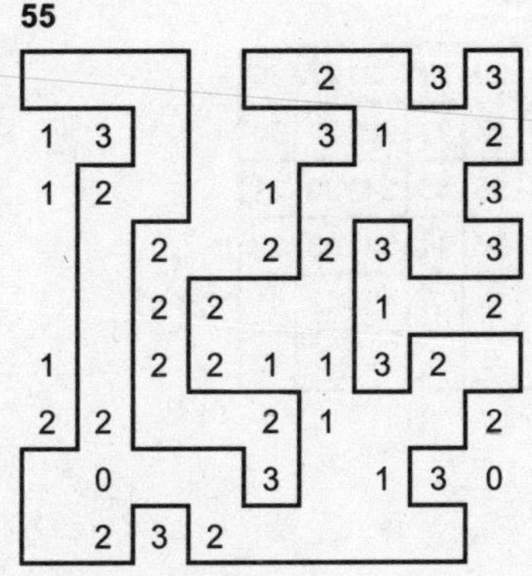

56

6	3	4	2	1	5
1	5	6	4	3	2
3	1	2	6	5	4
5	4	3	1	2	6
2	6	1	5	4	3
4	2	5	3	6	1

57

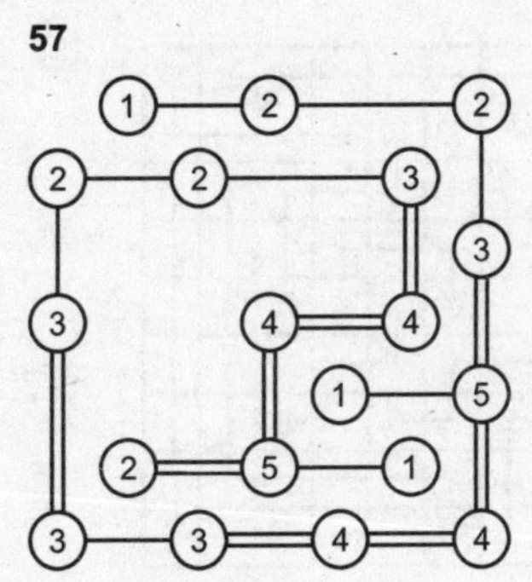

58

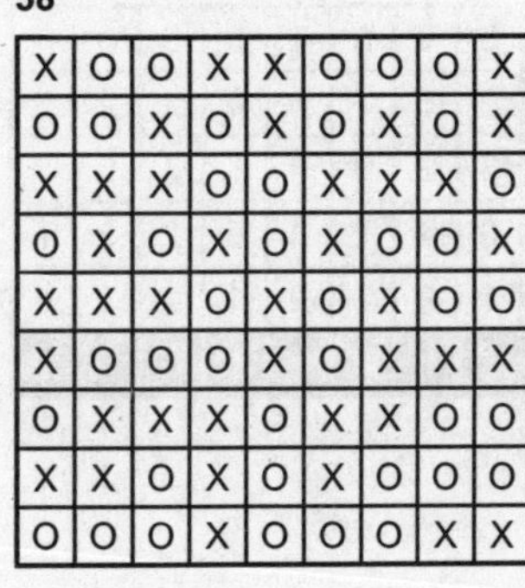

X	O	O	X	X	O	O	O	X
O	O	X	O	X	O	X	O	X
X	X	X	O	O	X	X	X	O
O	X	O	X	O	X	O	O	X
X	X	X	O	X	O	X	O	O
X	O	O	O	X	O	X	X	X
O	X	X	X	O	X	X	O	O
X	X	O	X	O	X	O	O	O
O	O	O	X	O	O	O	X	X

59

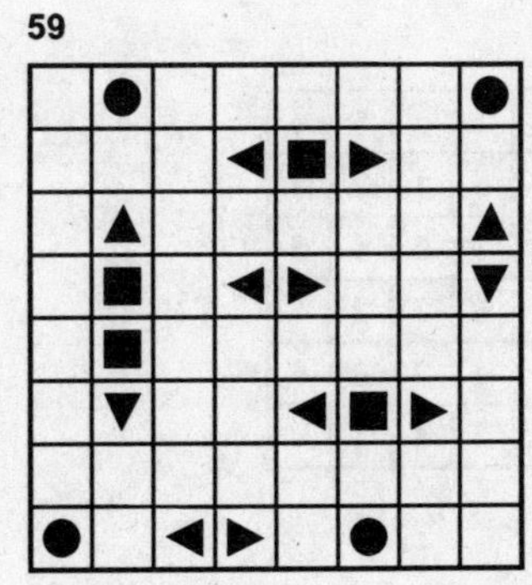

60

1	3	4	7	2	5	6
7	5	3	1	4	6	2
2	1	5	6	3	7	4
3	7	1	2	6	4	5
6	2	7	4	5	1	3
4	6	2	5	1	3	7
5	4	6	3	7	2	1

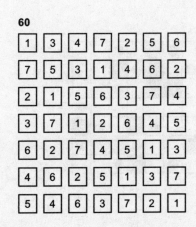

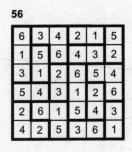

61

				0	1				
			0	2	5	3			
			6	1	3	0			
	6	6	6	5	3	6	3	1	
1	4	1	2	0	1	2	4	1	4
5	3	0	5	1	3	2	5	5	2
	3	2	0	6	3	4	0	4	
			0	2	6	4			
			4	5	2	5			
				6	4				

62

18	20	21	22	27	26
19	17	23	28	25	30
16	15	35	24	29	31
2	36	14	34	33	32
1	3	7	13	12	11
4	5	6	8	9	10

63

7	2	3	0	6	1	9	5	4	8
9	4	6	5	7	8	0	1	2	3
5	1	3	2	9	4	6	7	0	8
8	9	6	4	1	0	5	2	3	7
6	3	5	8	7	2	1	4	9	0
35	19	23	19	30	15	21	19	18	26

64

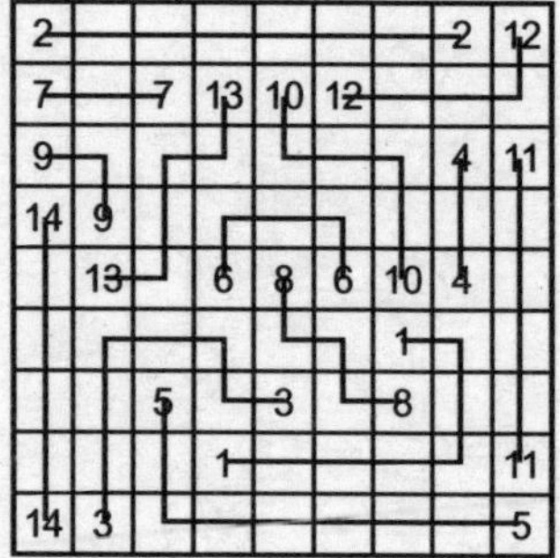

65

66

2	3	1	6	5	4
6	4	5	1	3	2
1	2	3	5	4	6
4	5	6	3	2	1
3	1	4	2	6	5
5	6	2	4	1	3

67

4	1	7	2	8	5	3	6
8	6	5	7	2	3	4	1
7	2	4	1	3	8	6	5
3	7	8	5	6	2	1	4
1	8	3	6	5	4	7	2
5	3	6	4	1	7	2	8
6	5	2	3	4	1	8	7
2	4	1	8	7	6	5	3

68

O	X	O	O	X	O	X	X
X	O	O	X	O	X	X	O
O	O	X	O	X	X	O	X
O	X	X	O	X	O	O	X
X	X	O	X	O	O	X	O
O	O	X	O	X	X	O	X
X	O	X	X	O	O	X	O
X	X	O	X	O	X	O	O

69

⬡ 1	○ 2	☆ 5	□ 3	◇ 4
○ 4	□ 1	◇ 3	☆ 2	⬡ 5
□ 5	☆ 4	⬡ 2	◇ 1	○ 3
☆ 3	◇ 5	○ 1	⬡ 4	□ 2
◇ 2	⬡ 3	□ 4	○ 5	☆ 1

70

B	F	D	C	A	E
A	C	E	D	F	B
E	B	C	F	D	A
C	D	A	B	E	F
D	E	F	A	B	C
F	A	B	E	C	D

71

△	□	△	□	○	△	□	△
□	○	□	△	□	□	○	□
○	△	○	△	△	□	△	○
□	○	△	□	○	○	□	□
△	□	○	□	□	○	△	□
□	○	□	○	△	□	○	△
○	△	○	△	□	○	△	△
○	□	○	○	△	□	○	□
○	□	□	△	△	□	□	△

72

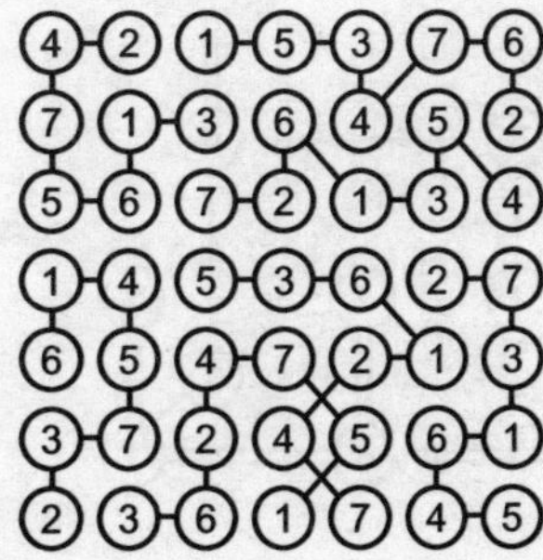

73

1	●	●	●	3	●		●	1
1		●	4	●			2	
		2		1	1		●	1
●		●	2		2		2	
2				●	●	3	●	1
●	1		3	●	●			
2			●	5	●	4	●	●
●	1	2	●		3	●		3
1				1		●	3	●

74

B	A	E	C	D	E	A	C	D	B
D	B	C	E	A	B	C	D	E	A
C	A	B	D	E	C	D	A	B	E
E	D	A	E	C	B	C	B	D	A
C	E	C	A	B	D	E	A	B	D
A	C	D	B	E	A	D	E	C	B
B	E	B	D	A	C	A	D	E	C
D	C	D	A	B	E	B	C	A	E
E	B	A	C	D	A	E	B	C	D
A	D	E	B	C	D	B	E	A	C

75

3	2	2	2			2		
2	2	3	2	3				0
3	2	2	1			3		1
	2	2	3		2		2	3
	2		2	1	3			
2	1						3	
	3		2			3		1
2		1	1		0	2		
	3	3	2		1	1		3

76

3	1	4	6	2	5
5	3	2	1	4	6
4	2	6	5	3	1
1	4	5	3	6	2
2	6	1	4	5	3
6	5	3	2	1	4

77

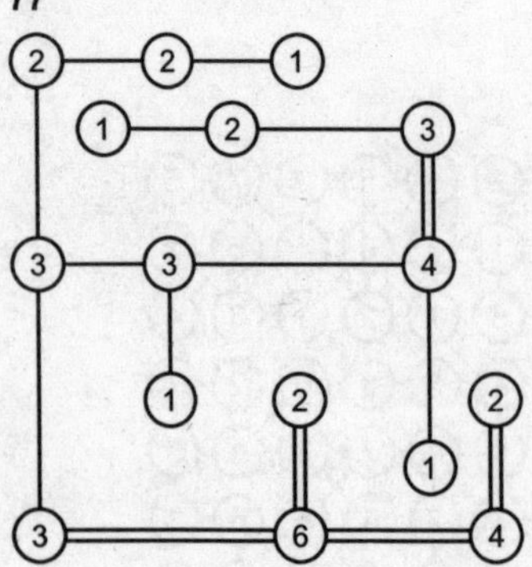

78

X	O	O	O	X	X	X	O	O	X
O	X	X	X	O	X	O	X	O	X
O	X	X	O	O	O	X	X	X	O
X	O	O	O	X	X	X	O	X	O
X	X	O	X	O	X	O	X	O	X
O	X	O	X	O	X	O	X	O	O
X	O	X	O	X	O	O	X	X	O
X	X	X	O	X	O	X	O	O	X
O	X	O	O	X	O	X	O	O	X
X	O	X	X	O	X	X	X	O	X
X	X	O	O	X	O	O	X	X	O

79

●								
		◀	■	▶			●	
●								
			▲				▲	
▲			■				▼	
■			▼					
■					▲			
▼			●		▼		◀	▶

80

5	7	6	1	3	2	4
1	6	2	4	5	3	7
3	1	7	5	2	4	6
4	3	5	2	7	6	1
6	5	1	3	4	7	2
2	4	3	7	6	1	5
7	2	4	6	1	5	3

81

6	6	3	2	2	0	5
5	6	3	1	3	2	4
3	2	6	4	2	3	4
6	4	1	1	2	0	4
0	0	5	0	0	1	0
2	6	6	5	1	4	5
4	3	1	5	5	2	0
1	1	3	4	5	6	3

82

12	11	3	2	39	42	41
13	10	4	38	1	40	43
14	9	37	5	48	44	46
8	15	6	36	49	47	45
16	7	20	27	35	34	33
17	19	26	21	28	31	32
18	25	24	23	22	29	30

83

8	4	2	7	6	9	0	1	5	3
0	5	6	9	3	8	4	2	7	1
1	2	4	7	6	0	3	9	8	5
4	6	3	5	2	9	8	1	0	7
9	1	8	6	3	0	7	5	4	2
8	2	0	1	7	4	9	6	3	5
30	20	23	35	27	30	31	24	27	23

84

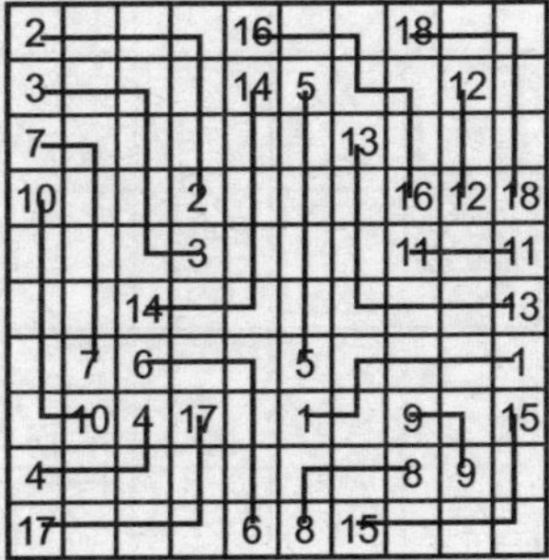

85

	1 (■)	■	●			
	●		3 (■)	●		
			●			
						●
	■	■				2 (■)
	0 (■)					●
●		■	■	1 (■)	●	

86

5	2	4	1	3	6
4	3	6	5	2	1
1	4	5	3	6	2
6	5	3	2	1	4
3	1	2	6	4	5
2	6	1	4	5	3

87

1	4	8	7	5	6	2	3
4	2	1	3	6	7	8	5
8	3	4	1	2	5	6	7
6	8	7	5	4	2	3	1
2	1	5	4	3	8	7	6
5	7	6	8	1	3	4	2
7	6	3	2	8	1	5	4
3	5	2	6	7	4	1	8

88

O	X	O	O	X	X	O	X
O	O	X	X	O	X	X	O
X	O	X	O	X	O	O	X
O	X	O	O	X	O	X	X
X	O	X	X	O	X	O	O
O	O	X	X	O	O	X	X
X	X	O	O	X	O	X	O
X	X	O	X	O	X	O	O

89

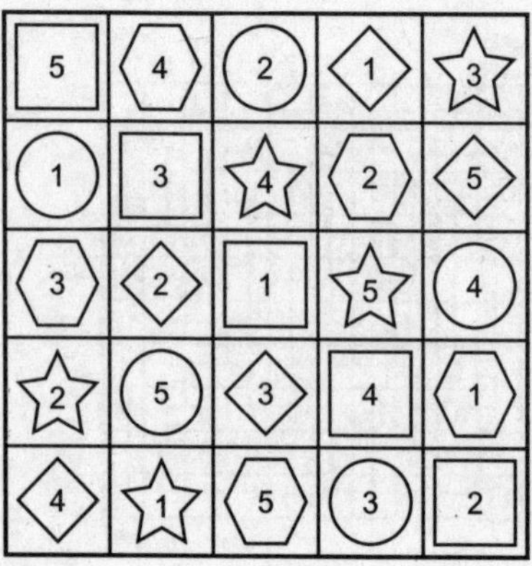

90

E	F	D	B	A	C
F	A	E	C	B	D
B	C	F	A	D	E
A	E	B	D	C	F
C	D	A	E	F	B
D	B	C	F	E	A

91

□	△	△	△	□	□	△	○
△	○	□	○	△	□	○	□
○	□	○	△	□	○	□	△
○	○	△	□	○	△	○	○
□	△	□	○	□	□	△	○
□	□	△	△	△	□	△	△
△	○	□	□	○	○	□	○
△	□	△	□	△	○	□	○
△	○	○	○	△	△	□	○

92

2	4	7	1	6	3	5
1	6	2	3	5	4	7
3	7	5	2	1	6	4
4	3	6	7	2	5	1
5	1	3	6	4	7	2
7	2	4	5	3	1	6
6	5	1	4	7	2	3

93

●	2	●	●	2	2	●	2	●
3			3	●	2			1
●	●	2		2		2	1	
3		●			●		●	
●	3	●	●	3		2		1
2			4	●		2		1
1	●	2		●	5	●	●	
2	2	3	●	5	●	●	●	2
●	1		●		●	4	2	

94

A	E	D	B	D	A	C	E	B	C
C	A	B	C	B	D	E	A	E	D
E	B	C	E	D	A	B	C	D	A
D	C	E	A	C	E	D	B	A	B
B	D	A	B	E	C	A	D	C	E
D	E	C	D	A	B	C	B	E	A
A	C	A	E	B	D	E	C	D	B
C	A	D	C	E	B	A	E	B	D
E	B	E	D	A	C	B	D	A	C
B	D	B	A	C	E	D	A	C	E

95

2		2	2	2	2			
			1	2	0	1	1	2
	1	3		3			1	1
1	3	2	1		3	1		0
1		3					1	
2		2	1	1		2		3
2		2		2				2
3	2			2	1		2	2
3		1		3	1	1		3

96

6	2	3	4	5	1
1	3	5	2	6	4
3	4	6	1	2	5
5	6	1	3	4	2
2	1	4	5	3	6
4	5	2	6	1	3

97

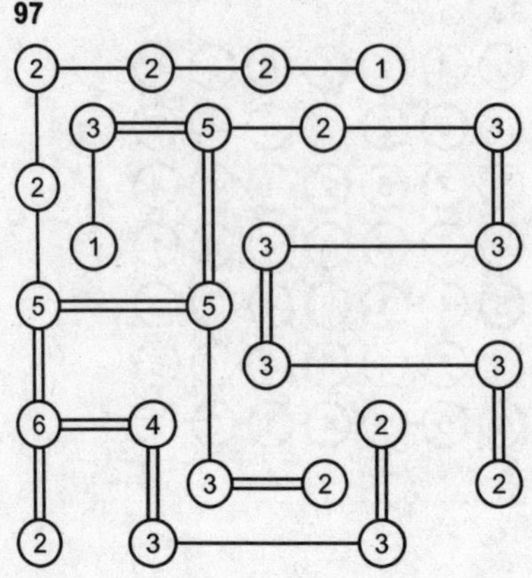

98

O	X	X	O	O	X	O	X	O	O
X	O	X	X	O	O	X	X	X	O
X	X	O	O	X	X	X	O	O	O
X	O	X	X	O	O	X	X	O	X
O	X	X	O	X	O	O	X	X	O
O	O	O	X	X	O	X	O	O	O
X	X	X	O	X	X	O	X	X	O
O	O	X	O	O	O	X	X	O	X
X	O	O	X	X	X	O	O	X	O
X	O	X	X	O	X	X	X	O	X
X	X	X	O	O	X	O	X	O	O

99

	◀	▶				●		●
	◀	■	■	▶			●	
	●		▲			▲		
			■			■		▲
◀	▶		▼			▼		▼

100

3	5	4	1	2	6	7
5	6	3	4	1	7	2
4	3	6	5	7	2	1
7	4	2	3	5	1	6
1	2	5	7	6	3	4
2	7	1	6	3	4	5
6	1	7	2	4	5	3

101

6	3	6	6	0	0	4
5	5	6	0	1	6	1
4	4	0	3	3	2	5
1	5	2	1	0	5	5
5	5	4	1	2	4	2
2	6	0	3	4	2	3
1	3	6	2	6	0	0
3	4	1	2	1	3	4

102

16	17	19	24	25	26	29
15	18	20	23	27	28	30
13	14	22	21	33	32	31
12	2	1	34	35	41	49
11	3	9	36	40	42	48
4	10	8	39	37	47	43
5	6	7	38	46	45	44

103

1	4	7	0	8	6	3	5	9	2
6	3	2	4	5	9	1	8	7	0
5	8	6	7	3	4	2	0	1	9
7	1	0	5	6	8	9	4	3	2
4	8	6	7	2	3	1	5	0	9
7	1	5	0	9	4	2	6	3	8
30	25	26	23	33	34	18	28	23	30

104

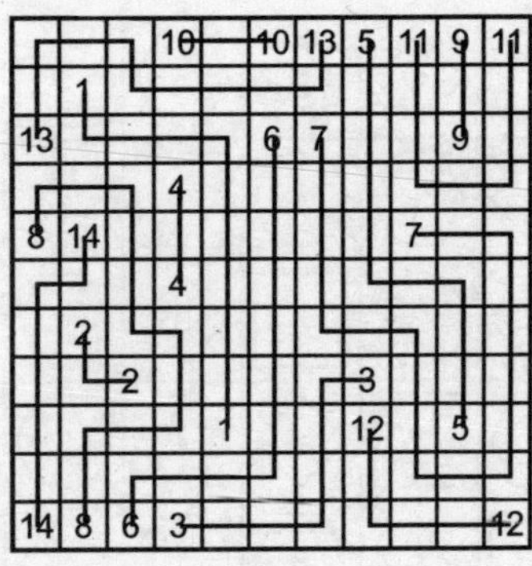

105

●			1	●			
2	●						
			●				
0	0			0		●	
		●					
●							
				●			
	●	2	●	3	●	2	●

106

2	1	5	6	4	3
3	5	4	2	6	1
4	3	2	1	5	6
5	6	3	4	1	2
6	4	1	3	2	5
1	2	6	5	3	4

107

8	7	3	6	2	1	4	5
7	8	5	2	1	3	6	4
3	2	6	1	4	5	8	7
2	1	8	4	7	6	5	3
6	5	4	7	3	8	2	1
5	6	1	3	8	4	7	2
4	3	2	5	6	7	1	8
1	4	7	8	5	2	3	6

108

X	O	O	X	O	O	X	X
O	O	X	O	X	X	O	X
O	X	X	O	O	X	X	O
X	O	O	X	X	O	X	O
O	X	X	O	X	O	O	X
O	O	X	X	O	X	O	X
X	X	O	X	O	O	X	O
X	X	O	O	X	X	O	O

109

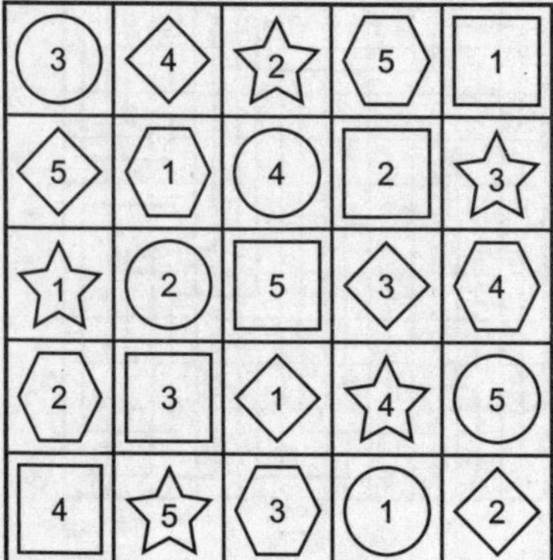

110

A	F	C	D	B	E
E	B	D	C	A	F
B	D	F	A	E	C
D	C	B	E	F	A
F	A	E	B	C	D
C	E	A	F	D	B

111

□	○	○	□	○	○	□	○
□	△	○	□	□	○	□	○
□	○	□	△	△	△	□	○
△	△	○	□	□	○	△	△
□	△	□	△	□	○	○	△
○	□	△	○	△	△	△	○
△	○	□	□	□	○	□	△
○	○	△	△	△	○	○	□
□	□	□	○	□	△	□	□

112

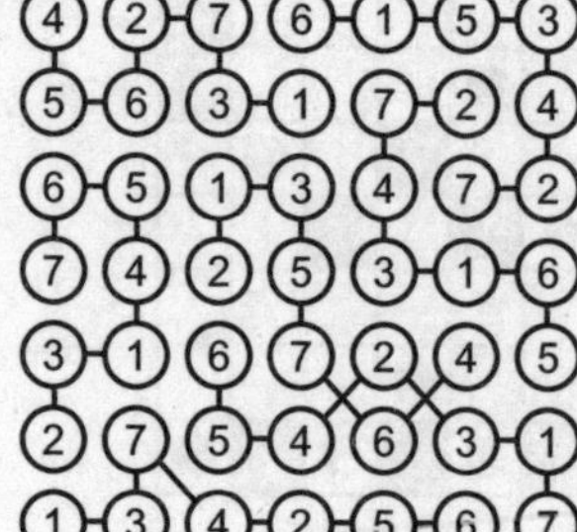

113

●	2	●	2	●	3	3	●	1
		2	4	4	●	●	4	
●	2	●	2	●	●	4	●	●
3		3						●
●	●		●	●		●		1
●	5		●	3		3	3	1
●	●	3	2			●	●	2
●	5	●	3		●	●	●	
2	●	3	●	●	●	4	2	

114

A	B	C	D	E	D	A	E	C	B
D	E	A	E	D	A	B	C	B	C
E	C	B	C	B	D	E	A	D	A
B	D	E	B	A	C	A	D	C	E
C	A	D	A	C	E	D	B	E	B
D	C	E	B	A	B	C	E	A	D
A	D	C	E	B	A	E	D	B	C
C	E	B	A	D	C	D	B	A	E
E	B	A	D	C	E	B	C	D	A
B	A	D	C	E	B	C	A	E	D

115

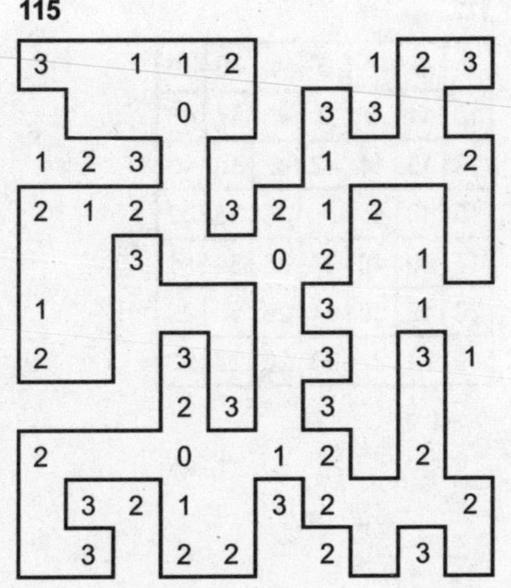

116

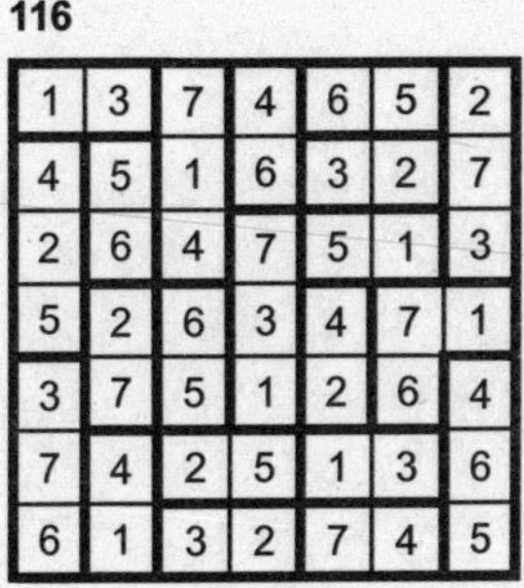

1	3	7	4	6	5	2
4	5	1	6	3	2	7
2	6	4	7	5	1	3
5	2	6	3	4	7	1
3	7	5	1	2	6	4
7	4	2	5	1	3	6
6	1	3	2	7	4	5

117

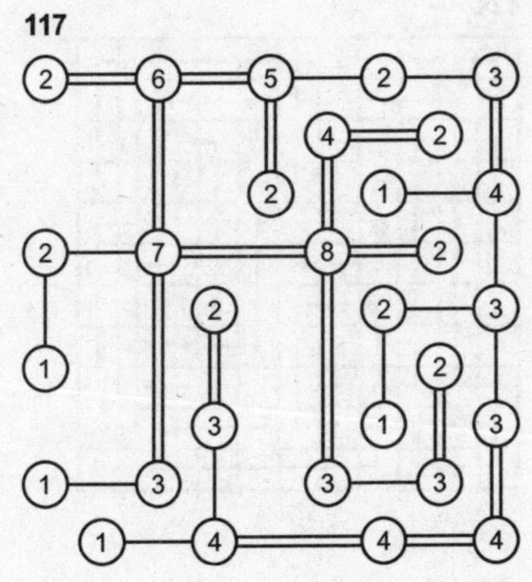

118

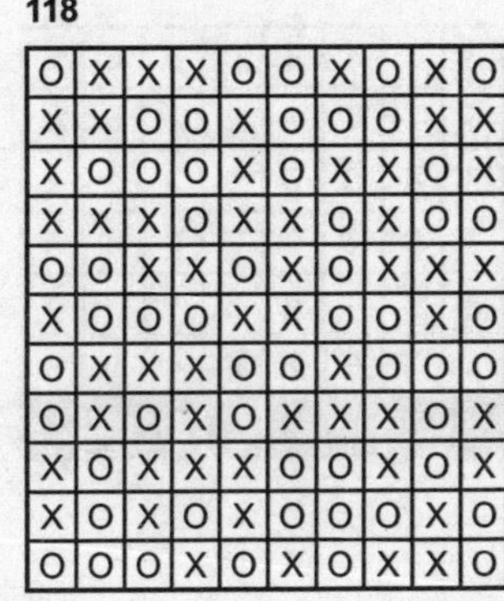

O	X	X	X	O	O	X	O	X	O
X	X	O	O	X	O	O	O	X	X
X	O	O	O	X	O	X	X	O	X
X	X	X	O	X	X	O	X	O	O
O	O	X	X	O	X	O	X	X	X
X	O	O	O	X	X	O	O	X	O
O	X	X	X	O	O	X	O	O	O
O	X	O	X	O	X	X	X	O	X
X	O	X	X	X	O	O	X	O	X
X	O	X	O	X	O	O	O	X	O
O	O	O	X	O	X	O	X	X	O

119

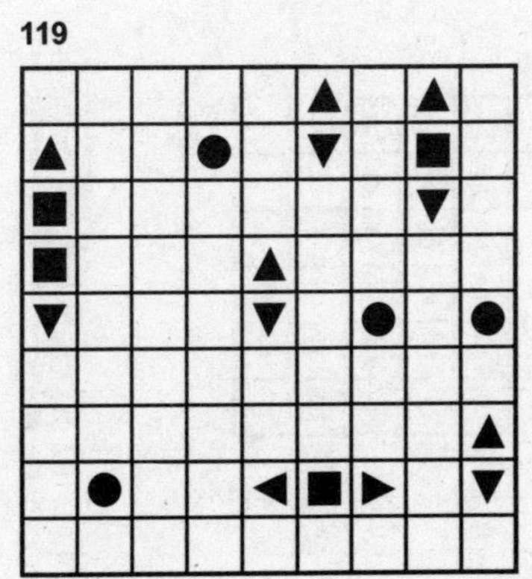

120

2	3	1	5	4	7	6
1	2	7	4	3	6	5
5	1	6	7	2	3	4
4	5	2	3	6	1	7
7	4	5	6	1	2	3
3	6	4	1	7	5	2
6	7	3	2	5	4	1

121

2	0	0	1	1	6	0
6	3	1	6	3	6	3
6	2	5	5	6	4	4
1	5	5	0	4	2	4
4	0	6	3	3	4	1
4	5	2	1	0	5	1
2	6	1	0	0	2	5
5	4	3	2	2	3	3

122

9	8	7	5	4	48	49
10	11	6	3	43	47	46
12	15	14	42	2	44	45
16	13	41	1	35	33	32
17	39	40	37	36	34	31
20	18	38	24	25	30	29
19	21	22	23	26	27	28

123

7	2	3	1	4	6	0	8	5	9
9	1	5	7	3	8	2	4	6	0
8	7	3	4	6	5	0	9	1	2
3	6	1	0	2	9	7	5	8	4
7	9	2	6	4	5	8	1	3	0
1	3	5	7	0	2	6	4	8	9
35	28	19	25	19	35	23	31	31	24

124

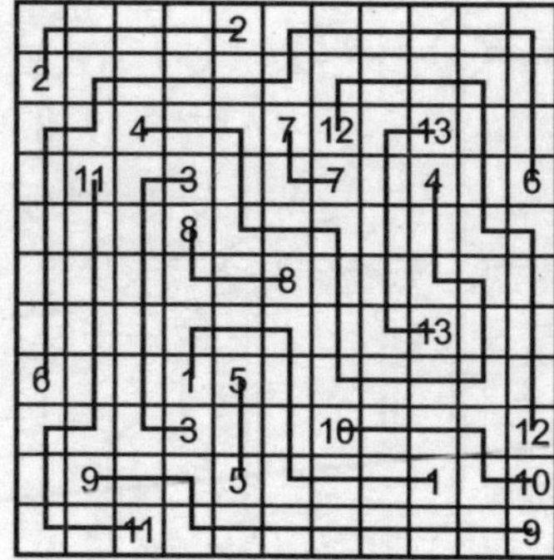

125

■	●			■ 1	●		
■	■		■ 0				■ 0
■						●	
				●			■ 0
■	●		■ 0			■	
						●	
		●	■ 2				●
			●		■ 0		■ 1

126

6	1	5	3	4	2
1	2	4	6	3	5
4	5	6	2	1	3
3	4	2	1	5	6
2	3	1	5	6	4
5	6	3	4	2	1

127

1	4	3	8	2	7	5	6
4	5	8	6	7	2	1	3
2	1	4	3	5	8	6	7
5	8	1	4	3	6	7	2
8	3	6	7	4	5	2	1
3	2	7	5	6	1	8	4
6	7	2	1	8	3	4	5
7	6	5	2	1	4	3	8

128

O	O	X	O	X	O	X	X
O	O	X	O	X	O	X	X
X	X	O	X	O	X	O	O
O	O	X	O	X	O	X	X
X	X	O	X	O	X	O	O
X	O	O	X	X	O	O	X
O	X	X	O	O	X	X	O
X	X	O	X	O	X	O	O

129

◇ 4	○ 1	□ 5	☆ 2	⬡ 3
○ 2	☆ 3	◇ 1	⬡ 5	□ 4
⬡ 1	□ 2	☆ 4	◇ 3	○ 5
□ 3	◇ 5	⬡ 2	○ 4	☆ 1
☆ 5	⬡ 4	○ 3	□ 1	◇ 2

130

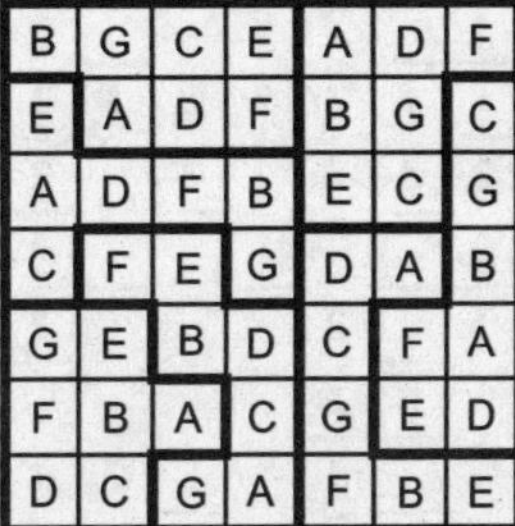

B	G	C	E	A	D	F
E	A	D	F	B	G	C
A	D	F	B	E	C	G
C	F	E	G	D	A	B
G	E	B	D	C	F	A
F	B	A	C	G	E	D
D	C	G	A	F	B	E

131

○	□	△	□	△	□	○	△	□
△	○	□	□	△	○	△	□	○
○	□	△	○	△	○	○	□	□
□	△	○	□	○	□	△	○	△
△	○	□	△	□	△	○	△	□
○	□	○	□	□	△	○	□	○
○	○	□	△	○	△	○	△	□
△	□	△	○	△	□	△	△	□
△	△	□	□	□	○	○	○	□

132

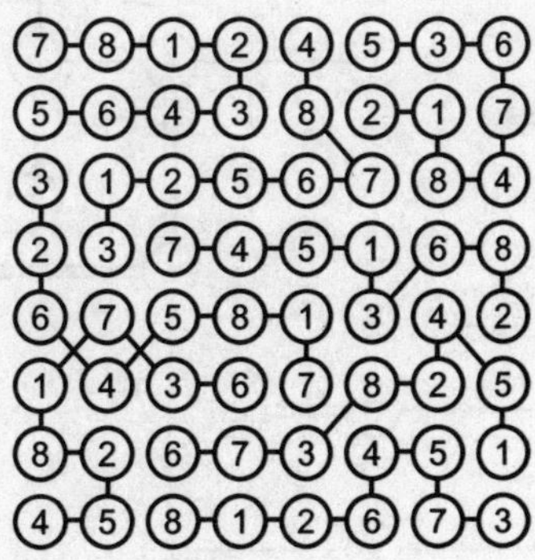

7	8	1	2	4	5	3	6
5	6	4	3	8	2	1	7
3	1	2	5	6	7	8	4
2	3	7	4	5	1	6	8
6	7	5	8	1	3	4	2
1	4	3	6	7	8	2	5
8	2	6	7	3	4	5	1
4	5	8	1	2	6	7	3

133

1		2	●		1	●	2		3	2
1	●		1			2		●	●	●
	2	2	1		●			3		2
2	3	●			2	●	3	●	4	
●	●	4	●	2	2	3		●	●	●
●	●		2		●	3	●	●	6	4
	3	●	1	3	●				●	●
1					●	●	●	3	4	●
●		●	1	2	●	5	3		●	2
2	4	2					●		3	
●		●	2	●	1	1		●	●	1

134

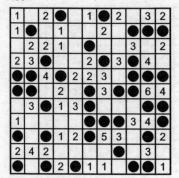

A	C	D	F	B	E	A	E	C	D	F	B
E	A	E	A	C	D	F	B	D	B	C	F
A	B	A	B	D	F	E	C	E	F	D	C
C	E	C	D	E	A	F	B	A	D	F	B
D	C	B	C	F	E	A	D	F	A	B	E
F	D	F	B	D	C	E	A	B	C	E	A
B	F	B	E	A	F	C	D	C	E	A	D
E	A	C	D	F	B	D	E	F	B	C	A
C	B	F	A	E	D	B	F	A	C	E	D
D	E	A	F	C	B	C	A	D	E	B	F
F	D	E	C	B	A	D	C	B	F	A	E
B	F	D	E	A	C	B	F	E	A	D	C

135

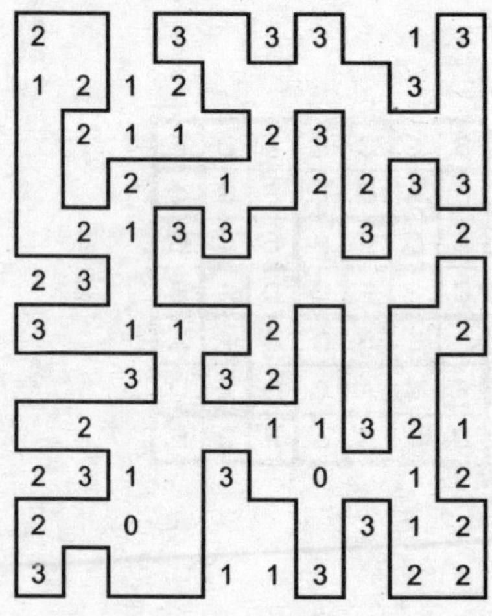

136

1	3	5	2	4	6	7	8
7	5	6	3	2	8	4	1
2	8	7	1	3	5	6	4
4	1	2	5	7	3	8	6
5	2	8	6	1	4	3	7
8	6	3	4	5	7	1	2
3	7	4	8	6	1	2	5
6	4	1	7	8	2	5	3

137

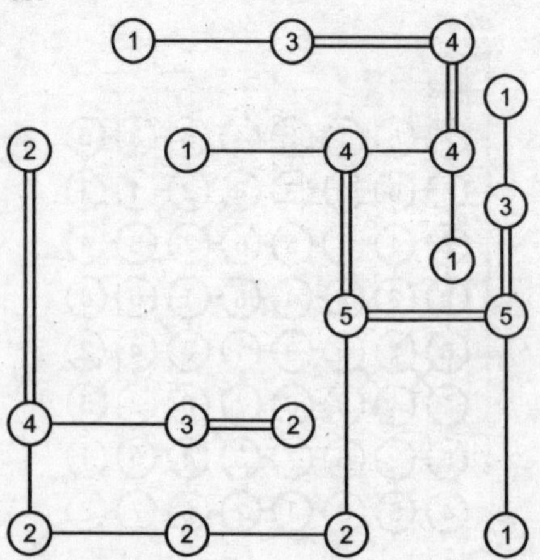

138

X	O	O	O	X	X	O	O	X	O
O	O	X	X	O	O	O	X	O	O
O	X	O	X	X	X	O	O	X	O
X	X	X	O	O	X	X	X	O	X
O	X	O	O	X	O	O	O	X	X
O	O	X	X	X	O	X	O	O	O
X	O	O	O	X	O	O	X	X	X
X	X	O	X	O	X	O	X	O	X
O	X	X	X	O	O	O	X	X	O
X	O	O	O	X	X	X	O	O	O
X	X	X	O	X	O	O	X	X	X
O	O	O	X	O	O	X	O	O	O
X	X	O	O	X	X	O	X	X	X

139

					●		▲	
		▲					■	
		■			●		▼	
▲		■						
▼		▼		●		◀	■	▶
						◀	▶	
		◀	▶					
							●	

140

6	7	3	2	8	5	4	1
2	5	1	6	4	3	7	8
7	8	4	1	6	2	5	3
5	2	6	7	3	8	1	4
1	3	7	5	2	4	8	6
8	4	2	3	1	7	6	5
3	1	8	4	5	6	2	7
4	6	5	8	7	1	3	2

141

4	0	4	4	5	6	7	4
0	2	2	1	4	0	5	1
6	7	7	5	3	3	5	2
4	7	3	0	3	1	1	0
3	6	2	5	7	0	6	5
6	1	3	2	5	1	4	2
5	0	0	6	7	2	4	3
7	1	5	2	6	7	0	1
6	6	3	4	1	3	2	7

142

24	23	22	30	20	32	33	1
27	25	29	21	31	19	2	34
26	28	55	15	16	18	3	35
52	54	50	56	14	17	4	36
53	51	57	49	39	13	37	5
60	59	58	40	48	38	12	6
64	61	41	43	44	47	11	7
62	63	42	45	46	10	9	8

143

8	4	2	1	5	7	3	6	0	9
6	5	0	7	2	1	9	4	8	3
8	7	2	6	4	3	5	1	0	9
2	3	9	8	5	7	0	4	6	1
5	1	7	3	4	6	2	8	9	0
0	6	9	8	2	7	3	5	4	1
29	26	29	33	22	31	22	28	27	23

144

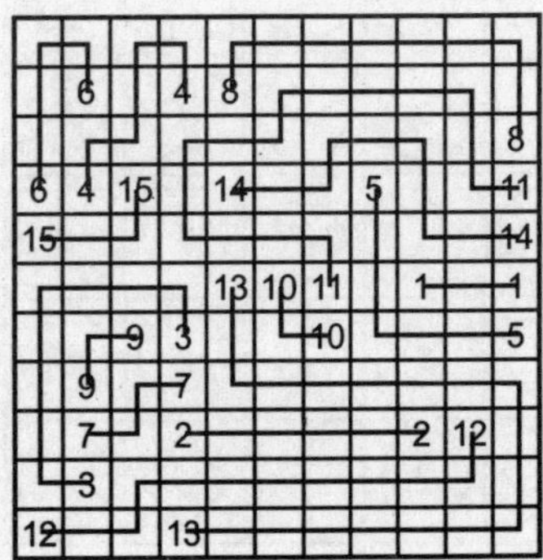

145

■ = shaded								
		●		■		●	■ 1	
■		■ 2		■ 0		■ 1		●
		●						■
			●			■ 1	●	
	●	■			●			
●	■ 2		■ 0			●		
■		●		■	■ 0			■
	●	■ 3	●					
●	■ 2				●	■ 1		●

146

1	7	4	5	3	2	6
7	5	1	3	2	6	4
3	4	5	1	6	7	2
4	2	6	7	1	3	5
2	1	7	6	4	5	3
6	3	2	4	5	1	7
5	6	3	2	7	4	1

147

4	1	5	2	6	7	9	8	3
5	2	9	4	7	8	3	1	6
9	8	2	5	3	6	7	4	1
1	4	7	6	9	3	2	5	8
2	9	3	8	1	4	5	6	7
7	5	4	9	8	1	6	3	2
8	3	6	1	5	2	4	7	9
3	6	1	7	2	5	8	9	4
6	7	8	3	4	9	1	2	5

148

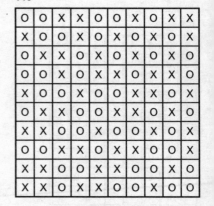

O	O	X	X	O	O	X	O	X	X
X	O	O	X	O	X	O	X	O	X
O	X	X	O	X	O	X	O	X	O
O	O	X	O	X	X	O	X	X	O
X	O	O	X	O	O	X	X	O	X
O	X	X	O	O	X	X	O	X	O
X	X	O	O	X	O	O	X	O	X
O	O	X	X	O	X	X	O	O	X
X	X	O	O	X	X	O	O	X	O
X	X	O	X	X	O	O	X	O	O

149

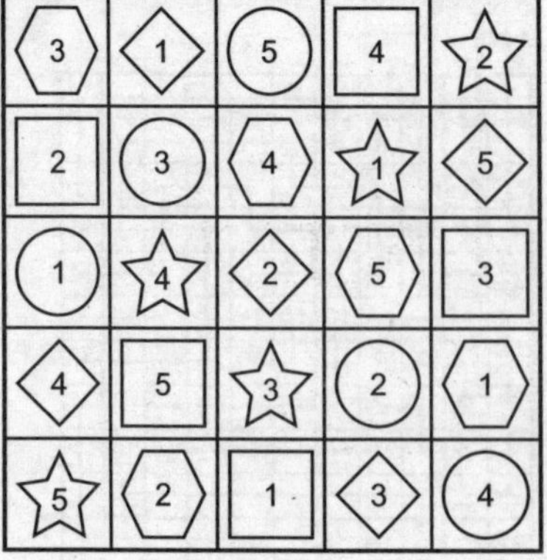

150

G	C	B	E	D	A	F
F	D	E	A	G	B	C
A	B	C	D	E	F	G
D	G	F	C	A	E	B
E	F	A	G	B	C	D
C	E	D	B	F	G	A
B	A	G	F	C	D	E

151

○	□	□	□	△	□	□	□	△
○	○	△	○	□	○	○	○	□
□	□	○	□	○	□	△	△	○
△	□	△	○	○	△	□	△	□
○	△	△	□	△	○	□	○	△
□	○	□	□	△	△	□	△	○
○	△	○	○	○	□	○	○	□
○	□	△	□	△	○	△	○	△
○	△	△	□	□	△	△	□	○

152

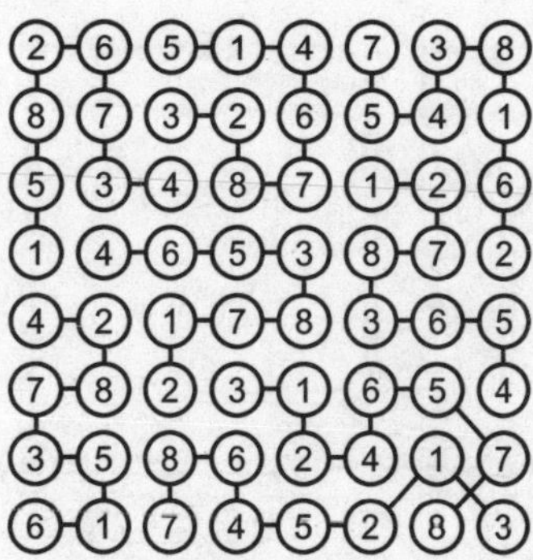

153

●	1		●	3			●	3	●	
		2	●	●	2	3	●		2	
1	1		2			●	2	1		●
2	●	3		1		3				1
●	3	●	●		2	●	●	2		1
2		3	●	●				●	3	●
●	2			●	3	1			4	●
●		1		3		●		1		●
	1		●	●			4	●		2
1		4	4			●	5	●	4	●
	●	●	●	1	2	●		●	3	1

154

F	D	E	C	F	B	A	C	D	E	A	B
D	A	F	D	B	C	E	F	A	B	C	E
B	F	C	A	D	E	B	A	F	C	E	D
E	B	A	C	E	D	F	D	C	A	B	F
A	E	F	A	C	B	D	B	E	D	F	C
C	A	B	E	F	D	C	E	B	F	D	A
F	C	D	B	E	A	F	A	C	D	B	E
C	D	B	E	A	F	C	F	D	B	E	A
D	E	C	F	B	A	D	C	E	F	A	B
B	C	E	D	A	F	E	D	B	A	C	F
E	B	A	F	D	C	A	B	F	E	D	C
A	F	D	B	C	E	B	E	A	C	F	D

155

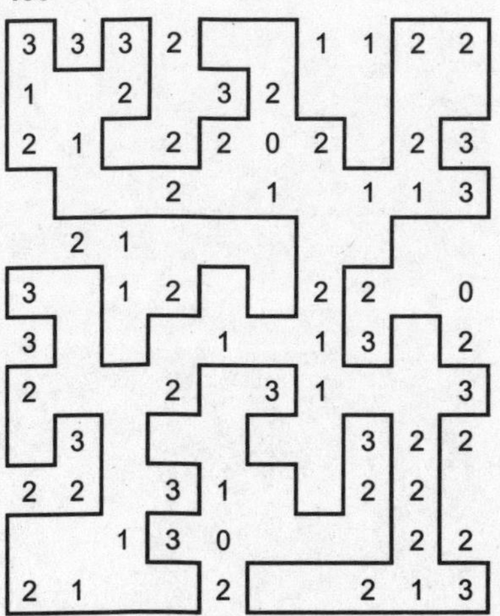

156

6	7	1	3	8	5	2	4
1	2	6	5	4	8	7	3
5	3	2	7	1	4	8	6
7	4	8	2	5	6	3	1
2	5	3	4	7	1	6	8
8	1	5	6	3	2	4	7
3	6	4	8	2	7	1	5
4	8	7	1	6	3	5	2

157

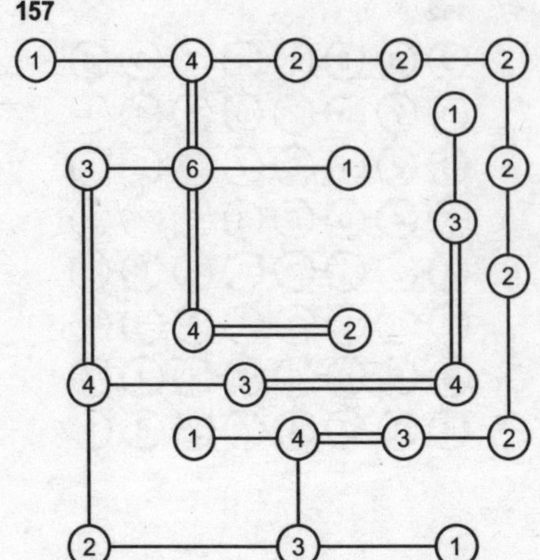

158

O	X	X	O	O	X	O	X	X	X
O	X	O	X	X	O	X	O	X	O
X	O	X	O	O	O	X	O	O	O
X	X	O	X	X	O	O	X	X	X
O	X	X	X	O	X	O	X	O	O
X	X	X	O	O	O	X	X	X	O
O	O	X	O	X	O	O	O	X	O
X	O	O	O	X	X	O	X	X	X
O	X	X	X	O	O	O	X	O	X
X	X	O	O	X	X	X	O	O	X
O	O	X	X	O	O	O	X	O	O
X	O	O	O	X	X	X	O	X	X
X	O	O	O	X	O	X	X	O	O

159

		●						
				▲			▲	
◀	■	▶		▼			■	
							■	
							▼	
●		◀	■	▶				
							◀	▶
	●		▲					
			▼					●

160

7	1	3	6	8	4	5	2
5	6	1	7	4	2	8	3
3	8	6	2	7	5	1	4
8	3	4	1	5	6	2	7
1	4	2	5	3	8	7	6
6	2	7	8	1	3	4	5
4	7	5	3	2	1	6	8
2	5	8	4	6	7	3	1